BACKGROUND TO THE GOSPEL OF ST. MARK

D1711279

RUDOLF STEINER

Background to the Gospel of St. Mark

Thirteen lectures given in Berlin, Munich, Hanover and Coblenz, between 17th October, 1910 and 10th June, 1911

Translated by E. H. Goddard and D. S. Osmond

1968
RUDOLF STEINER PRESS, LONDON
ANTHROPOSOPHIC PRESS, INC., NEW YORK

First Edition 1923
Second Edition 1937
Third Edition 1968
(a completely new translation with additions)
Reprinted 1985

The translation has been made from shorthand reports unrevised by the lecturer. The original German texts are published in the Complete Edition of the works of Rudolf Steiner with the title: *Exkurse in das Gebiet des Markus-Evangeliums* (No. 124 in the *Bibliographical Survey*, 1961).

 This English edition is published by permission of the *Rudolf Steiner Nachlassverwaltung,* Dornach, Switzerland.

Cover design by Christiana Beaven

ISBN 0 85440 660 3
ISBN 0 88010 145 8

Printed in Great Britain by
Billing & Sons Ltd, Worcester

The following lectures were given by Rudolf Steiner to audiences familiar with the general background and terminology of his anthroposophical teaching. It should be remembered that in his autobiography, *The Course of my Life*, he emphasises the distinction between his written works on the one hand and, on the other, reports of lectures which were given as oral communications and were not originally intended for print. For an intelligent appreciation of the lectures it should be borne in mind that certain premises were taken for granted when the words were spoken. 'These premises,' Rudolf Steiner writes, 'include at the very least the anthroposophical knowledge of Man and of the Cosmos in its spiritual essence; also what may be called "anthroposophical history", told as an outcome of research into the spiritual world.'

*　　　*　　　*　　　*

The lectures contained in this volume had been preceded by courses given by Rudolf Steiner on the Gospels of St. John, St. Luke and St. Matthew and are to be regarded as a preparation for the more specialised course on the Gospel of St. Mark which was given more than a year later, when the necessary basis for an approach to its particular mysteries had been created. The present course, consisting of ten lectures, was given in Berlin under the title, *Exkurse in das Gebiet des Markus-Evangeliums,* and in this volume the texts of two other lectures and notes of a third given in other cities have been added. This will explain the repetitions in the later lectures.

*　　　*　　　*　　　*

A list of publications in English translation relevant to the themes of the following lectures, and a summarised plan of the Complete Edition of Rudolf Steiner's works in the original German will be found at the end of the present volume.

CONTENTS

ON THE INVESTIGATION AND COMMUNICATION OF SPIRITUAL TRUTHS

Now that we are resuming activities in the Berlin Group it is well to think for a short time of the studies in which we have been engaged since last year.

You will remember that about a year ago, in connection with the General Meeting of the German Section, I gave a lecture to the Berlin Group with the title: *The Sphere of the Bodhisattvas.** In that lecture on the mission of the Bodhisattvas in the world my purpose was to introduce the subject to which our main attention was to be directed in the Group meetings last winter. Our study was concerned with the Christ-problem, particularly in relation to the Gospel of St. Matthew and also in relation to the Gospels of St. John and St. Luke. And I indicated that at some later date we should be preparing for a still deeper study of the Christ-problem in connection with the Gospel of St. Mark.

In these studies we were not attempting a mere exposition of the Gospels. I have often spoken of this in perhaps rather extreme terms, and made it clear that Spiritual Science would still have been able to describe the events in Palestine even if there had been no historical records of them. The real authority for what we have to say about the Christ Event is

* When the present lecture-course was given, Rudolf Steiner was the General Secretary of the German Section of the Theosophical Society. His association with that Society was terminated in 1912 by its President, Mrs. Annie Besant, largely on account of the difference in his teaching on Christianity and the nature of the Second Coming, and the official founding of the Anthroposophical Society took place in Berlin, in 1913. The lecture on the Bodhisattvas is printed as the first in the Course entitled: *The Christ Impulse and the Development of Ego-consciousness.*

not to be found in any written document but in the eternal, spiritual record known as the Akasha Chronicle, decipherable only by clairvoyant consciousness. I have often explained what this really means. We compare what has first been learned from spiritual investigations with what is recorded in the Gospels or in other New Testament sources about the events in Palestine. And in the end we recognise that in order to read the Gospel records as they should be read, we must first—without reference to them—have investigated the mysteries connected with the happenings in Palestine, and that precisely because of this independent approach the value we attach to the Gospels and the reverence we feel for them, greatly increase.

But if we take into account not only the immediate interests of our present gathering but also the fact that contemporary culture needs a new understanding of the recorded sources of Christianity, we shall expect Spiritual Science not merely to satisfy our own intellectual difficulties about the events in Palestine but also to translate into the language of present-day culture what it says about the significance of the Christ Event for the whole evolution of humanity. It would not do to limit ourselves to the contributions made in previous centuries towards an understanding of the problem and the figure of Christ. If that were sufficient for the cultural needs of the modern age we should not find so many people unable to reconcile their sense of truth with accepted Christian tradition and who in one way or another actually repudiate the accounts of the events in Palestine as they have been handed down and believed in for centuries. All this makes it clear that modern culture needs a new understanding, a new enunciation, of the truths of Christianity.

Among many other aids to the investigation of Christian truths one is particularly effective. It consists in extending our vision and our feeling and perception beyond the horizons within which, in recent centuries, man has had to seek an understanding of the spiritual world. Here is a simple indication of how these horizons can be widened.

Goethe—to take as an example this master-spirit of recent European culture—was, as we all know, a man of titanic genius. Many studies have helped us to understand what depths of spiritual insight lay in Goethe's personality and to see that we ourselves can attain a high level of spiritual understanding through contemplating the texture of his soul. But however good our knowledge of Goethe may be, however deeply we steep ourselves in what he has to offer, there is something we shall not find in him, although it is essential if our vision is to be broadened in the right way and our horizon widened for our most urgent spiritual needs. There is no indication that Goethe had any inkling of certain things we can learn about and benefit from to-day— I mean, the concepts of the spiritual evolution of humanity which first became accessible to us in the nineteenth century through interpretations of documentary records of the spiritual achievements of the East. We there find many concepts which, far from making an understanding of the Christ-problem more difficult, if rightly applied help us to realise the nature of Christ Jesus. I therefore believe that there could be no better introduction to the study of the Christ-problem than an exposition of the mission of the Bodhisattvas—as they are named in Oriental philosophy. They are the great spiritual Individualities whose task it is from time to time to influence evolution. In Western culture there had for centuries been no knowledge of concepts such as that of the Bodhisattvas: yet only by mastering such concepts can we acquire some measure of knowledge of what Christ has been for mankind, what He can be and will continue to be.

So we find that study of an extensive phase of the spiritual development of mankind can be fruitful for the civilisation and culture of our own time. From another point of view as well it is important, when reviewing past centuries, to emphasise clearly the difference between men living at the turn of the nineteenth and twentieth centuries and men living in the eighteenth or nineteenth centuries, as well as the fact that until about a century ago very little was known in Europe about Buddha and Buddhism. Finally, we must remember that the impulse leading to the goal of our endeavours is the feeling we have when we confront great spiritual truths. For what really matters is not so much the knowledge that someone may wish to acquire, but rather the warmth of feeling, the power of perception, the nobility of will, with which his soul confronts the great truths of humanity. In our Groups the prevailing tone and atmosphere are more important than the actual words spoken. These feelings and perceptions vary greatly but the most important of all is reverence for the great truths and the feeling that we can approach them only with awe and veneration; we must realise that we cannot hope to grasp a great reality through a few concepts and ideas casually acquired and co-ordinated.

I have often said that we cannot accurately visualise a tree that is not actually in front of us if we have drawn a sketch of it from one side only, but that we must go round it and sketch it from many different sides. Only by assembling these different pictures can we obtain a complete impression of the tree. This analogy should make clear to us what our attitude should be to the great spiritual truths. We can make no progress at all in any real (or apparent) knowledge of higher things by approaching them from one side only. Whether or not there is truth in the particular view we may hold, we should always be humble enough to recognise that all our ideas are, and cannot help being, one-sided. If we intensify such a feeling of humility we shall welcome all ideas which throw light on any possible aspect of the great facts of existence. The age in which we are living makes this necessary, and the necessity will be increasingly borne in upon us. Consequently we no longer shut ourselves off from other views or from paths to the supreme truths which may differ from our own or from that of contemporary thought. During the course of the last few years, in considering the fruits of Western culture, we have tried always to maintain the principle of true humility in knowledge. I have never had the audacity to attempt to give one single survey of the events which comprise what we call the Christ-problem. On the contrary, I have always said that we were approaching the problem now from one point of view, now from another. And I have always emphasised that not even then has the problem been exhausted but that much further patient work is necessary.

The reason for studying the four Gospels separately is that we can then approach the Christ-problem from four different standpoints. We find that the four Gospels do, in fact, present four different aspects, and we are reminded that this stupendous problem must not be approached from one side only but at least from the four directions of the spiritual heavens indicated by the names of the four Evangelists: Matthew, Mark, Luke and John. If this is done we shall come increasingly to understand the problems and the great truths which are needed for the life of the human soul; and on the other hand, we shall never say that the one form of truth we may have grasped is the whole truth.

All our studies this last winter have been directed towards evoking a mood of humility in knowledge. Indeed without such humility no progress in the spiritual life is possible. Again and again I have laid stress upon the basic qualities essential for any progress in spiritual knowledge, and anyone who has followed the lectures given here week by week will confirm this.

Progress in spiritual knowledge—this is of course one of the basic impulses of our Movement. What does it mean to the soul? It fulfils the soul's worthiest needs and longings and provides the support which everyone conscious of his true humanity requires. Moreover this support is completely in line with the intellectual needs of the present day.

The progress in knowledge made possible by Spiritual Science should throw light on things which cannot be investigated by our ordinary senses but only by the faculties which belong to man as a spiritual being. The great questions about man's place in the physical world and what lies beyond the manifestations of the senses in this world, the truths concerning what lies beyond life and death—these questions meet a profound need, indeed the most human of all needs, of man's soul. Even if for various reasons we hold aloof from these questions and succeed for a time in deceiving ourselves by maintaining that science cannot investigate them, that the necessary faculties do not exist, nevertheless in the end the need and longing to find answers to them never disappear. The origin of what we see developing in the course of childhood and youth, the destination of what lies harboured in our soul as our bodily constitution begins to wilt and wither, in short, how man is connected with a spiritual world—these questions arise from a deep human need and man can dispense with the answers to them only when he deceives himself about his true nature.

But because these questions spring from so deep a need, because the soul cannot live in peace and contentment if it does not find the answers, it is only natural that people should look for an easy, comfortable way of finding them. Although many people would like to deny it, these questions have become particularly urgent in every domain of life, and what a variety of paths to the answers are offered to us! It can be said without exaggeration that the path of Spiritual Science is the hardest of them all. Many of you will admit that some of the sciences to-day are very difficult, and you will hesitate to tackle them because you are frightened by what you will have to master if you are really to understand them. The path of Spiritual Science may appear to be easier than, let us say, that of mathematics or botany or some other branch of natural science. Yet in the strictest sense the path of Spiritual Science is more difficult than that of any other science. This can be said without exaggeration. Why, then, does it seem easier to you? Only because it stirs the interests of the soul so forcefully and makes so compelling an appeal. It may be the most difficult of all the paths along which man is led into the spiritual world to-day, but we should not forget that it will lead to the highest within us. Is it not natural that the path to the highest should also be the hardest? Hence we should never be frightened by or blind to the inevitable difficulties of the path of Spiritual Science.

Among many features of this path, one has repeatedly been mentioned here. A person wishing to follow it must, to begin with, seriously imbibe what spiritual investigation has already been able to present about the mysteries and realities of the spiritual world. Here we touch upon a very important chapter of progress in Spiritual Science. People speak glibly about a spiritual science that cannot be corroborated, about spiritual facts alleged to have been witnessed and investigated by some initiate or seer, and they ask: Would it not be better simply to show us how we can quickly make our own way upwards into regions from which to glimpse the spiritual world? Why are we constantly told: This is what it looks like, this is how it appears to such and such a seer? Why are we not shown how to make the ascent quickly ourselves?

There are good reasons why facts which have been investigated about the spiritual world are communicated in general terms before details are given of the methods of training whereby the soul itself can be led into those higher spheres. We gain something very definite if we apply ourselves reverently to the study of what spiritual investigations have revealed from the spiritual world. I have often said that the facts of the spiritual world must be investigated and can be discovered *only* by clairvoyant consciousness; but I have as often said that once someone possessed of clairvoyant consciousness has observed these facts in the spiritual world and then communicates them, they must be communicated in such a way that even without clairvoyance, everyone will be able to test them by reference to the normal feeling for truth present in every soul, and by applying to them his own unprejudiced reasoning faculties. Anyone endowed with genuine clairvoyant consciousness will always communicate the facts about the spiritual world in such a way that everyone who wishes to test what he says will be able to do so without clairvoyance. But at the same time he will communicate them in a form whereby their true value and significance can be conveyed to a human soul.

What, then, does this communication and presentation of spiritual facts mean to the soul? It means that anyone who has some idea of conditions in the spiritual world can direct and order his life, his thoughts, his feelings and his perceptions in accordance with his relationship to the spiritual world. In this sense every communication of spiritual facts is important, even if the recipient cannot himself investigate those facts with clairvoyant consciousness. Indeed for the investigator himself these facts acquire a human value only when he has clothed them in a form in which they can be accessible to everyone. However much a clairvoyant may be able to see and investigate in the spiritual world, it remains valueless both to himself and to others until he can bring the fruits of his vision into the range of ordinary cognition and express them in ideas and concepts which can be grasped by a natural sense of truth and by sound reasoning. In fact, if his findings are to be of any value to himself he must first have understood them fundamentally; their value begins only at the point where the possibility of reasoned proof begins.

There is a radical test which can be applied to what I have just said. Among many other valuable spiritual truths and communications you will certainly attach very great importance to those concerning what a man can take with him through the gate of death of the spiritual truths he has assimilated on the physical plane between birth and death. Or, to put it differently: How much remains to a man who, by cultivating the spiritual life, has mastered the substance of communications relating to the spiritual world? The answer is: Exactly as much remains to him as he has fundamentally grasped and understood and has been able to translate into the language of ordinary human consciousness.

Picture to yourselves a man who may have made quite

exceptional discoveries in the spiritual world through clairvoyant observation but has never clothed them in the language of ordinary life. What happens to such a man? All his
discoveries are extinguished after death; only so much remains of value and significance as has been translated into
language which, in any given period, is the language of a
healthy sense of truth.

It is naturally of the greatest importance that clairvoyants
should be able to bring tidings from the spiritual world and
make them fruitful for their fellow-men. Our age needs such
wisdom and cannot make progress without it. It is essential
that such communications should be made available to
contemporary culture. Even if this is not recognised to-day,
in fifty or a hundred years it will be universally acknowledged
that civilisation and culture can make no progress unless
men become convinced of the existence of spiritual wisdom
and realise that humanity must die unless spiritual wisdom is
assimilated. And even if all space were conquered for the
purposes of intercommunication, mankind would still have to
face the prospect of the death of culture if spiritual wisdom
were rejected. This is true beyond all shadow of doubt.
Insight into the spiritual world is absolutely essential.

In addition to the value of spiritual wisdom for single
individuals after death there is its value for the progress of
humanity on the Earth. To have the right idea here, distinction must be made between the clairvoyant who has been
able to investigate the spiritual world and express his findings in terms of healthy human reason, and a man whose
karma while he was incarnated made it impossible for him to
see into the spiritual world, and who had consequently to
rely upon hearing from others about the findings of spiritual
research. What is the difference between the fruits enjoyed
after death by two such individuals? How do the effects
of spiritual truths differ in an Initiate and in one who knows
them only by hearsay and cannot himself see into the
spiritual world? Is the Initiate better off than a man who
could only hear these truths from someone else?

For humanity in general, vision of spiritual worlds is, of course, worth more than absence of vision. A seer is in touch with those worlds and can teach and help forward the development not only of men but of spiritual beings as well. Clairvoyant consciousness, then, is of special value. For the individual, however, knowledge alone has value and in this respect the most gifted clairvoyant is not to be distinguished from one who has merely heard the communications without being able in the present incarnation to look into the spiritual world himself. Whatever spiritual wisdom we have assimilated will be fruitful after death, no matter whether or not we ourselves are seers.

One of the great moral laws of the spiritual world is here presented to us. Admittedly, our modern conception of morality may not be subtle enough to understand its implications fully. No advantage is gained by individuals— except perhaps a merely selfish gratification—because their karma has made it possible for them to see into the spiritual world. Everything we acquire for our individual life must be acquired on the physical plane and must be moulded into forms appropriate to that plane. If a Buddha or a Bodhisattva stands at a higher level than other human individualities among the hierarchies of the spiritual world, it is because he has acquired these higher qualities through a number of incarnations on the physical plane.

Here is an indication of what I mean by the higher morality, the higher ethics, resulting from the spiritual life. —Let nobody imagine that he gains any advantage over his fellow-men through developing clairvoyance, for that is simply not so. He makes no progress which can be justified on any ground of self-interest. He achieves progress only in so far as he can be more useful to others. The immorality of egoism can find no place in the spiritual world. A man can gain nothing for himself by spiritual illumination. What he does gain he can gain only as a servant of the world in general, and he gains it for himself only by gaining it for others.

This, then, is the position of the spiritual investigator among his fellow-men. If they are willing to listen to him and assimilate his findings, they make the same progress as he does. This means that spiritual achievement must be employed only to further the general well-being of man, and not for any selfish purposes. There are circumstances when a man is moral not merely of his own volition but because immorality or egoism would be of no advantage. It is also easy to realise that there are dangers in penetrating into the spiritual world without proper preparation. By leading a spiritual life we do not achieve anything which will fulfil a selfish purpose after death. On the other hand, a man may wish to gratify an egotistic purpose in his life on Earth through spiritual development. Even if nothing egotistic can benefit existence in the spiritual world, there may be a wish to fulfil some egotistical purpose on the Earth.

Most people who follow the path leading to higher development are likely to say that they will obviously strive to discard egoism before trying to enter the spiritual world. But believe me, there is no province of life where deception is likely to be as great as it is among those who claim that their endeavours are free from egotistic interests. It is easy enough to say this, but whether it can be a fact is quite another matter. It is a different matter because when a man begins to practise exercises which can lead him into the spiritual world, he then, for the first time, confronts himself as he truly is. In ordinary life very few things are experienced in their true form. A man lives in a web of ideas, of impulses of will, of moral perceptions and conventional actions, all of which originate in his environment, and he seldom stops to ask himself how he should act or think in a given case if his upbringing had not been what it was. If he were to answer this question honestly, he would realise that his shortcomings are very much greater than he has assumed them to be.

The result of practising exercises through which a man learns how to rise into the spiritual world is that he grows beyond the web woven around him through custom, education,

environment. He quickly grows beyond all this. In soul
and spirit he is stripped naked. The veils with which he has
clothed himself and to which he clings in his ordinary feelings and actions, fall away. This accounts for a quite common phenomenon of which I have often spoken.—Before
beginning to work at his spiritual development a man may
have been a reasonable, possibly also a very intelligent and
at the same time, humble person who went through life
without committing any particular stupidities. Then, after
beginning this development, he may become arrogant and
do all sorts of senseless things. He seems to have lost his
bearings in life. To those familiar with the spiritual world
the reason for this is clear. If we are to maintain balance and
a sense of direction in face of what comes to the soul from the
spiritual world, two things are necessary. It must not make us
giddy or light-headed. In physical life our own organism
protects us through what we call in anthroposophical
lectures, the 'sense of balance or equilibrium'. Just as in a
man's physical body there is something which enables him to
keep himself upright—for if the organism is not functioning
properly he will get giddy and may fall down—so in the
spiritual life there is something which helps him to orientate
himself in his relation to the world, and this he must be able
to do. Spiritual unsteadiness comes about because what used
to support him, namely the external world and his own
sense-perceptions, fall away and he has then to rely upon
himself alone. The supports have gone and there is a danger
of giddiness. When the supports fall away we may easily
become arrogant, for arrogance is always latent in us
although it may not previously have disclosed itself.

How, then, can we attain the necessary spiritual balance or
equilibrium? We must assimilate with diligence, perse-
verance and dedication the findings of spiritual research
which have been expressed in terms harmonising with our
normal sense of truth and sound reasoning. It is not out of
caprice that I emphasise so repeatedly how necessary it is to
study what we call Spiritual Science. I emphasise it not in

order that I may have opportunity to speak here often but it is the only thing which can give the firm support we need for spiritual development. Earnest, diligent assimilation of the results of Spiritual Science is the antidote for spiritual 'giddiness' and insecurity. And anyone who has experienced this insecurity through having followed a wrong path of spiritual development—although he may think he has been very diligent—should recognise that he has failed to take in what can flow from Spiritual Science. The study of spiritual-scientific facts from every possible aspect—that is what is necessary for us. And that was why, last winter—though our ultimate purpose was to bring home the significance of the Christ Event for humanity—emphasis was laid over and over again upon the fundamental conditions for spiritual progress.

If a man is to make such progress there must be purpose and direction in his life of soul; but he needs something else as well. The soul can indeed acquire assurance through the study of Spiritual Science but it also needs a certain spiritual strength and courage. Courage of the kind necessary for spiritual progress is not essential in ordinary life because from the time of waking to that of going to sleep, our inmost being of soul-and-spirit is embedded in our physical and etheric bodies; and during the night we are inactive and can do no harm. If a man spiritually undeveloped were capable of acting during sleep as well as during waking life, he could do a great deal of harm. But in our physical and etheric bodies there are not only the forces which are active in us as conscious beings, or as thinking and feeling beings, but also those forces at which divine-spiritual Beings have worked through the evolutionary periods of Old Saturn, Old Sun, Old Moon and the Earth itself. Forces from higher spheres are continually active in us and support us. On waking from sleep we give ourselves up to the divine-spiritual Powers which, for our well-being and blessing, are present in our physical and etheric bodies and lead us through life from morning till evening. Thus the whole spiritual world is active within us; we can do harm to it in many respects but very little to make amends for the damage we have done.

All spiritual development depends upon our inner being, that is to say, our astral body and Ego, becoming free; we have to learn to become clairvoyant in the part of ourselves that is unconscious during sleep, and because it is unconscious can do no harm. What is unconscious in the members of our constitution in which divine-spiritual forces are active, must become conscious. All the strength we have because on waking we are taken in hand by spiritual powers anchored in our physical and etheric bodies, falls away when we become independent of those bodies and clairvoyant perception begins. We withdraw from the forces which have been a buttress for us against the influences working from the external world; but that world remains as it was and we still confront the whole power of its impact. If we are to resist this impact we must develop in our Ego and astral body all the power we otherwise draw from the physical and etheric bodies. This can be achieved if we follow the indications given in my book, *Knowledge of the Higher Worlds and its Attainment*. The aim of all these indications is to impart to our inmost self the strength previously bestowed by higher Beings, the strength which falls away when we lose the external supports provided by our physical and etheric bodies.

Individuals who have not made themselves inwardly strong enough to replace the powers they have discarded when they become independent of the physical and etheric bodies through serious training of the soul—above all through purifying the quality designated as immorality in the external world—these individuals may still be able to acquire faculties enabling them to see into the spiritual world. But what happens then? They become over-sensitive, hyper-sensitive. They feel as if from every side they are being spiritually buffeted and cannot stand up against the blows rained on them from all sides. One of the important facts to be realised by anyone who aspires to make progress in

spiritual knowledge is that inner strength must be developed
through the cultivation of the noblest and finest qualities of
the soul.

What are these qualities? Egoism will not help us in the
spiritual world and indeed makes it impossible to exist there.
Naturally, then, the best preparation for the spiritual life is
to banish egoism and everything which stimulates selfish
prospects of spiritual progress. The more earnestly we adopt
this principle the better are our prospects for spiritual progress. Anyone who has to do with these things will often hear
a man say that his action was not prompted by egoism.
But when such a man is on the point of letting words like this
pass his lips, he should check them and admit to himself that
he is not really able to insist that there is no trace of egoism
in his action. To admit it is much more intelligent, simply
because it is more truthful. And it is truth that matters whenever self-knowledge is concerned. In no realm does un-
truthfulness bring such severe retribution as in the realm of
spiritual life. A man should demand truth of himself instead
of claiming to be without egoism. At least if we acknowledge
our egoism we have a chance to get rid of it!

In regard to the concept of spiritual truth, let me say this.
There are people who claim to have seen and experienced
all kinds of things in the higher worlds—things which are
then made public. If we know that these things are not
true, should we not use every possible means to oppose
them? Certainly, there may be points of view according to
which such opposition is necessary. But those whose main
concern is truth have a different thought, namely that only
what is true can flourish and bear fruit in the world and
what is untrue will quite certainly be unfruitful. Put more
simply, this means that however much people may lie about
spiritual matters, what they say will not get very far, and
they should recognise that nothing fruitful can be achieved
by lies. In the spiritual world, truth alone will bear fruit;
and this holds good from the very beginning of our own
spiritual development, when we must admit to ourselves

what we really are. The conviction that truth alone can be fruitful and effective must be an impulse in all occult movements. Truth justifies itself by its fruitfulness and by the blessings it brings to mankind. Untruths and lies are always barren. They have only one result which I cannot go into in any further detail now; I can only say that they react most violently against those who actually spread them abroad. We shall consider on some other occasion what this significant statement implies.

I have tried to-day to give a kind of review of the activities in our Groups during the past year and to recapture the mood and tone which permeated our souls.

In speaking of the work carried on outside the Groups during the past year, I may perhaps mention my own participation which culminated in the production in Munich of the Rosicrucian Mystery Play, *The Portal of Initiation*. Later Group meetings will give us an opportunity of explaining what was then attempted. For the present I will merely say that in the Play it was possible to give a more artistic and individual form to what could otherwise be expressed in a more general way. When we speak here or anywhere else of the conditions of the spiritual life, we speak of them as they concern every soul. But it must always be borne in mind that each man is an individual whose soul must be studied individually. Consequently it was essential that one particular soul should be depicted at the threshold of Initiation. The Rosicrucian Mystery Play is accordingly to be regarded not as a manual of instruction but as an artistic representation of the preparation for Initiation of a particular individual, *Johannes Thomasius*.

In our approach to truth we have thus reached two important standpoints. We have presented the general line of progress and have also penetrated to the heart of an individual soul. We are always conscious of the fact that truth must be approached from many sides and that we must wait patiently until its different aspects merge into a single picture. We shall adhere faithfully to this attitude of humility in knowledge. Let us not say that man can never experience truth. He assuredly can! But he cannot know the whole truth at once; he can know only one side. This makes for humility in knowledge and true humility is a feeling that must be cultivated in our Groups and carried into the general culture of the day, for the whole character of our age needs such an attitude.

In this spirit we shall continue our task of presenting the Christ-problem, in order to learn from it how to achieve real humility in knowledge and thereby make further and further progress in the experience of truth.

HIGHER KNOWLEDGE AND MAN'S LIFE OF SOUL

In the last lecture I gave a survey of our studies during the past year and an indication of the purpose and spirit of those studies. I said that the whole spiritual-scientific Movement must be permeated by the same spirit which actuates our study, for instance, of the many aspects of the Christ-problem. In all our striving for knowledge we must display modesty and humility and it is of this humility that I want to speak a little more specifically.

I have often said that while an object can be depicted in some way by painting or photographing it from one side, it must never be claimed that such a picture is in any sense a complete presentation. We can get an approximate idea of an object if we look at it from several sides and gather the single pictures into one whole, but even in ordinary observation we have to go all round an object if we want to get a comprehensive idea of it. And if anyone were to imagine that he could obtain the whole truth about some matter relating to the spiritual world from a single glimpse of that world, he would be greatly mistaken. Many errors arise from failure to recognise this. The four accounts of the events in Palestine given by the four Evangelists are actually a safe-guard against students taking such an attitude. People who do not know that in spiritual life an object or a being or an event must be contemplated from different sides will, with their superficial approach to truth, find apparent contra-dictions in the accounts of the individual Evangelists. But it has been repeatedly pointed out that the four accounts present the great Christ Event from four different aspects and that they must be viewed as a whole, just as we should have to do in the case of an object painted from four different sides.

If we proceed with careful attention to detail, as we have tried to do in connection with the Gospels of St. Matthew. St. Luke and St. John and later on shall try to do with that of St. Mark, we shall see that there is wonderful harmony in the four accounts. The mere fact that there are four Gospels is a sufficient indication of the need to look at truth from four different sides.

During the past year I have often spoken of the possibility of discovering different aspects of truth. At our General Meeting last year I tried to supplement what is usually called 'Theosophy' by another view which I called that of 'Anthroposophy' and I showed how it is related to Theosophy. I spoke of a science based upon physical facts and upon the intellectual assessment of facts revealed to sense-observation. When this science deals with Man, we call it Anthropology, which comprises everything about Man that can be investigated by the senses and studied by means of rational observation. Anthropology, therefore, studies the human physical organism as it presents itself to the methods and instruments used by natural science. It studies the relics of prehistoric men, the tools and implements used by them and since buried in the earth, and then tries to form an idea of how the human race has evolved through the ages. It also studies the stages of development in evidence among savages or un-civilised peoples, starting from the assumption that these peoples are now at the stage of culture attained by civilised humanity in much earlier times. In this way Anthropology forms an idea of the various stages through which man has passed before reaching his present level.

A great deal more could be said to shed light on Anthro-pology. Last year I compared it to a man who gains his knowledge of a country by walking about on flat ground, noting the market-towns, the cities, woods and fields, and describing everything just as he has seen it from the flat countryside.

But there is a different point of view from which man can be studied, namely that of Theosophy. The ultimate aim of

Theosophy is to shed light upon the *nature and purpose of man.*
If you study my book, *Occult Science*, you will see that everything culminates in a description of man's true being. If
Anthropology can be compared with a man who collects his
facts and data by walking about on flat ground and then
tries to understand them, Theosophy can be compared with
an observer who climbs to a mountain-top and from there
surveys the surrounding country, looks at the market-
towns, the cities, the woods, and so on. Much that he sees on
the ground below will be unclear and often he will see particular points only. The standpoint adopted by Theosophy
is on a lofty level at which many of the qualities and idio-
syncracies displayed by man in daily life become unclear,
just as villages and towns are indistinct when they are viewed
from the top of a mountain.

What I have just said will not, perhaps, be very enlightening to someone who is only beginning his study of Spiritual
Science. He will try to understand and form certain ideas of
the nature and being of man, of the physical, etheric and
astral bodies and so on, but at first he will not come up
against the difficulties that lie ahead when he tries to make
progress in the deeper understanding of Spiritual Science.
The greater the progress he makes, the more he recognises
how difficult it is to find a connection between what has
been attained on the heights of Spiritual Science and the
feelings and perceptions of daily life.

Someone might ask why it is that spiritual truths seem
illuminating and right to many people in spite of the fact
that they are incapable of testing what they have been told
from spiritual heights by comparing it with their own observations in everyday life. The reason is that there is an
affinity between the human soul and truth. This instinctive,
natural sense of truth is a reality and of untold value particularly in our own day, because the spiritual level from
which essential truths can be seen is so infinitely high. If
people had first to scale these heights themselves they would
have a long road in the life of soul and spirit to travel and

those unable to do so could have no sense of the value these truths have for human life. But once spiritual truths have been communicated, every soul has the capacity to assimilate them.

How is a soul which accepts these truths to be compared with one which is able actually to discover them? A trivial analogy can be chosen here, but trivial as it is it means more than appears on the surface.—All of us can put on our boots, but not all of us can make them; to do that we should have to be bootmakers. What we get out of the boots does not depend upon being able to make them but upon being able to put them to proper use.—This is precisely the case with the truths given us through Spiritual Science. We must apply them in our lives, even though we cannot ourselves discover them as seers. When we accept them because of our natural feeling for truth they help us to orientate our lives, to realise that we are not limited to existence between birth and death, that we bear within us a spiritual man, that we pass through many earth-lives, and so on. These truths can be absorbed and applied. And just as boots protect us from the cold, so do these truths protect us from spiritual cold and from the spiritual poverty we should experience if we were capable of thinking, feeling and perceiving only what the external sense-world presents to us. Spiritual truths are brought down from the heights for the use and benefit of all human beings, though there may be only a few who can actually find them, namely those who have trodden the spiritual path already described.

Any view of the world around us—which, when it is a question of studying Man is also the concern of Anthropology—shows us how this world itself reveals behind it another world which can be observed from the higher, spiritual standpoint of Theosophy. The sense-world itself can reveal another world if we do not just accept the facts with the intellect, but interpret them; when, that is to say, we do not move so far beyond the field of sense-perception as does Theosophy itself but stand as it were on the mountain-side where a wider view is possible without the details becoming unclear. This standpoint was characterised last year as that of Anthroposophy, showing that three views of Man are possible, namely the views of Anthropology, of Anthroposophy and of Theosophy.

This year, in connection with our General Meeting, the lectures on 'Psychosophy'—which will be as significant as those on Anthroposophy, only in a quite different sense— will show how, on the basis of its impressions and experiences, the human soul itself can be described in its relation to spiritual life. Later lectures on 'Pneumatosophy' will conclude this series and will show how our studies of Anthroposophy and Psychosophy merge into Theosophy. The aim of all this is to show you how manifold truth is. The earnest seeker discovers that the further he progresses, the humbler he becomes and also the more cautious in translating into the language of ordinary life the truths attained at higher levels. For although it has been said that these truths acquire value only when they are thus translated, we must realise that this translation is one of the most difficult tasks of Spiritual Science. There are very great difficulties in making what has been observed at high levels of the spiritual world intelligible to a healthy sense of truth and acceptable to sound reasoning.

It must be emphasised again and again that when Spiritual Science is studied in our Groups the object is to create this feeling for truth. We have not merely to grasp with the intellect what has been communicated from the spiritual world; it is much more important to experience it in our feelings and so acquire qualities which everyone who strives earnestly for spiritual truth should possess.

As we look at the world around us we can say that at every point it displays to us an outer manifestation of an inner, spiritual world. For us this is now a commonplace. Just as a man's physiognomy is an expression of what is going on in his soul, so all phenomena of the external sense-world are a physiognomical expression, so to speak, of a spiritual world behind them. We understand sense-percep-

tions only when we can see in them expressions of the spiritual
world. When by following his own path to knowledge a man
cannot reach the stage at which spiritual vision is possible, he
has only the material world before him, and he may ask
whether his study of the material world provides any confirmation, any evidence, of communications based upon
spiritual vision.

This search for evidence is always possible but it will have
to be carried out with precision and not superficially. If, for
example, you have followed my lectures and have read the
book *Occult Science*, you will know that there was a time when
the Earth and Sun were one, when Earth and Sun formed
one body. If you bear in mind what I have said, you will
agree that the animal forms and plant forms on the Earth
to-day are later elaborations of those already in existence
when the Earth and the Sun were one. But just as the animal
forms of to-day are adapted to the conditions prevailing on
the present Earth, so must the animal forms of that earlier
epoch have been adapted to the conditions of the planetary
body of Earth plus Sun. It follows that the animal forms
which have survived from those times are not only survivors
but developments of creatures which were already then in
existence but could not, for instance, have possessed eyes: for
eyes have purpose only when light is streaming in upon the
Earth from outside, from the Sun. Accordingly, among the
different creatures belonging to the animal kingdom there
will be some which developed eyes after the Sun had separated from the Earth, and also animal forms which are survivors from the time when Sun and Earth were still united.
Such animals will have no eyes. They would naturally
belong to the lower species of animals. And we find that such
creatures actually exist. Popular books tell us that animals
below a certain stage of evolution have no eyes. This is
confirmed by Spiritual Science.

The world around us, the world in which we ourselves live,
can therefore be pictured as the 'physiognomical' expression
of the spiritual life weaving and working behind it. If man

were simply confronted by this sense-world and it did not anywhere reveal to him that it points to a spiritual world, he could never feel longing for that world. There must be a point in the sense-world where a longing for spiritual reality springs up, some point where the spiritual streams as through a door or window into the world of our everyday life. When does this happen? When does a spiritual reality light up in us? As you will know from lectures given by me and by others as well, this happens when we experience our own 'I', our own Ego. At this moment we actually do experience something that has a direct relation with the spiritual world. Nevertheless this experience of the 'I' is at the same time very meagre. It is as it were a single point amid all the phenomena of the world. The single point which we express by the little word, 'I', does indeed indicate something truly spiritual but this has contracted into a point. What can we learn from this spiritual reality that has contracted into the point, into the 'I'? Through experiencing our own 'I' we can know no more of the spiritual world than has contracted into this single point unless we widen the experience. Nevertheless this point does contain something of great importance, namely that through it we are given an indication of the process of cognition that is necessary for knowledge of the spiritual world.

What is the difference between experience of the 'I' and all other experiences? The difference is that we are ourselves actually *within* the experience of the 'I'. All other experiences come to us from outside.

Someone may say: 'But my thinking, my willing, my desires, my feelings—I myself live in all that.' In regard to willing, however, a man can convince himself by a very simple act of introspection that he cannot be said to be actually within it. The will is something that seems to be driving us on, as if we were not within it; our actions seem to be due to the pressure of some thing or some incident from outside. And it is the same with our feelings and with most of our thoughts in everyday life. How little we are really within our thinking in everyday life can be realised if we try conscientiously to note how dependent it is upon education, upon the conditions we have encountered in life. This is the reason why human thinking, feeling and willing vary so greatly in different nations and in different periods. Only one thing remains the same in all nations, in all regions and in all societies: it is the *experience of the 'I'*.

Let us now ask in what this experience of the 'I' really consists. The matter is not as simple as it might appear. You may easily think, for instance, that you experience the 'I' in its real nature. But this is by no means so. We do not actually experience the 'I' itself but only a mental concept, a mental picture, of it. If we could really experience the 'I', it would present itself as something raying out on all sides to infinity. Unless the 'I' could confront itself as an image in a mirror, even though the image is only a point, we could not experience the 'I', nor could the 'I' create a mental picture of itself. What man experiences of the 'I' is a mental picture of it; but that is sufficient, for it differs entirely from every other picture in that it is identical with its original. When the 'I' makes a mental picture of itself it is concerned with itself alone and the picture is only the return of the 'I' experience into itself. There is a kind of obstruction, as if we wished to check the experience and compel it to return into itself; and in this return it confronts itself as a mirror-image. Such is the experience of the 'I'.

It can therefore be said that we recognise the experience of the 'I' in the mental picture of it. But this mental picture of the 'I' differs radically from all other mental pictures, all other experiences which we may have. For all other mental pictures and all other experiences we need something like an organ. This is obvious in the case of outer sense-perceptions. In order to have the mental picture of a colour we must have eyes. It is quite obvious that we must have organs through which ordinary sense-perceptions reach us. You may think that no organ is necessary for what is so intimately related to our inmost self. Here too, however, you can quite easily convince yourselves that you do need an organ. You can find more precise details in my lectures on Anthroposophy; at the moment I am making it possible for you to hear in theosophical terms what was presented in those lectures rather for the benefit of the general public.

Suppose that at some period in your life you grasp a thought, an idea. You understand something that confronts you in the form of an idea. How can you understand it? Only through those ideas which you have previously mastered and made your own. You can see that this is so from the fact that when a new idea comes to a man it is accepted in one way by one person and differently by another. This is because the one person has within him a greater number of ideas than the other. All our old ideas are lodged within us and confront the new idea as the eye confronts the light. A sort of organ is formed from our own previous ideas; and for anything not formed in this way in the present incarnation we must look to earlier incarnations. This organ was formed then and we confront new ideas with it. We must have an organ through which to receive all experiences that come to us from the outer world, even when they are spiritual experiences: we never stand spiritually naked, as it were, in face of what comes to us from the external world, but we are always dependent upon what we have become. The only time we confront the world directly is when we attain a perception of the 'I'. The 'I' is always there, even while we sleep, but perception of it has to be aroused every morning when we wake up. If during the night we were to journey to Mars, the conditions surrounding us would certainly be very different from those on the Earth—indeed everything would be different—*except* the perception of the 'I'. This is always the same because no external organ is needed for it, not even an organ for concepts. What confronts us here is a direct perception of the 'I' in its true form. Everything else comes before us as a picture in a mirror and conditioned by the structure of the mirror. Perception of the 'I' comes to us in its own intrinsic form.

In fact we can say that when we have a mental picture of the 'I', we are ourselves within it and it is in no sense outside us. And now let us ask how this unique perception of the 'I' differs from all other perceptions. The difference lies in the fact that in the perception, the mental picture of the 'I', there is the *direct* imprint of the 'I', and in no other perception is this the case. But from everything around us we get pictures which can be *compared* with the perception of the 'I', for through the 'I' we transform everything into an inner experience. If we are to see any meaning or significance in the external world it must become a mental picture in us. Thus we form pictures of the external world which then live on in the 'I', no matter which organ is the channel for a sense-experience. We may smell some substance; when we are no longer in direct contact with it we still carry an image within us of the smell. The same is true of a colour we have seen; the pictures or images which come from such experiences remain in our 'I'. The characteristic feature of all these pictures or images is that they come to us from outside. All the pictures which, as long as we live in the world of the senses, we have been able to unite with our 'I', are the relics of impressions received from the sense-world. But there is one thing the sense-world cannot give us— namely, perception of the 'I'. This arises in us quite spontaneously. Thus in perception of the 'I' we have a picture which rises up within ourselves, contracted into a point.

Think now of other mental pictures which have not arisen from any external stimulus given by the senses but arise freely in the 'I' like the concept of the 'I' itself, and are consequently formed in the same manner. Images and pictures of this kind arise in the *astral world*. There are, then, mental pictures which arise in the 'I' without our having received any impression from outside, from the sense-world.

What distinguishes the images or pictures we derive from the sense-world from the rest of our inner experiences? Images derived from the sense-world can remain with us as images of experiences only after we have come into contact with that world; they become *inner* experiences although they were stimulated by the outer world. But what experiences of the 'I' are there that are *not* directly stimulated by the outer world? Our feelings, desires, impulses, instincts and so on, are such experiences. Even if we ourselves are not actually within these feelings, impulses, etc., in the sense already described, it must nevertheless be admitted that there is something which distinguishes them from the images that remain with us as a result of what our senses have perceived.—You can feel what the difference is. An image derived from the outer world is something that is at rest within us, that we try to retain as faithfully as possible. But impulses, desires and instincts represent something that is active within us, something that is an actual force.

Now although astral pictures arise without the external world having played any part, something must nevertheless have been in action, for nothing can exist as an effect without a cause. What causes a sense-image is the impression made by the outer world. What causes an astral picture is what lies at the root of desires, impulses, feelings, and so on. In ordinary life to-day, however, man is protected from developing in his feelings a force strong enough to cause pictures to arise which would be experienced in the same way as the picture of the 'I' itself. The significant feature of modern man's soul is that its impulses and desires are not strong enough to create a picture of what the 'I' sets before them. When the 'I' confronts the strong forces of the external world it is stimulated to form pictures. When it lives within itself, in a normal man it has only one single opportunity of experiencing an emerging picture, namely, when the picture is that of the 'I' itself.

Impulses and desires are therefore not strong enough to create pictures comparable with the 'I'-experience. If they are to work strongly enough they must acquire a certain quality, a most important quality that is inherent in all sense-experiences. Sense-experiences do not behave just to suit us: if, for instance, someone lives in a room in which he hears an irritating noise, he cannot get rid of it by means of his impulses and desires. Through a mere impulse or desire nobody can turn a yellow flower into a red one because he prefers it. It is characteristic of the sense-world that its manifestations are quite independent of us. This is certainly not true of our impulses, desires and passions which are entirely consonant with our personal life. What, then, must happen to them in the process of intensification that is necessary to make them into pictures? They must become like the external world which does not consult our wishes in regard to its structure and the production of sense-images but compels us to give to the image we make the form imparted to it by the surrounding world.

If pictures of the astral world are to be correctly formed a man must be as detached from himself, from his personal sympathies and antipathies, as he is from sense-images he forms of the outer world. What he desires or wishes must be a matter of complete indifference to him. In the last lecture I said that this requirement simply means the complete absence of egoism. But this must not be taken lightly. It is no easy matter to be without egoism.

The following must also be borne in mind. Our interest in what comes to us from the outside world is vastly different from our interest in what arises within ourselves. The interest a man takes in his inner life is infinitely greater than his interest in the external world. You certainly know people who, when they have transformed something in the external world into an image, are apt to make it conform with their subjective feelings. Such people often spin the wildest yarns even when they are not actually lying, and believe what they say. Sympathy and antipathy always play a part here and create delusions about the external reality, causing the subsequent image to be distorted. But these are exceptional cases, for a man would not get very far if he were himself to create delusions in his daily life. There would be perpetual clashes with the circumstances of outer existence, but willy-nilly he is bound to acknowledge the truth of the external

world; reality itself puts him right. It is the same with
ordinary sense-experiences: the external reality is a sound
corrective. This is no longer the case when a man begins to
have inner experiences: it is not so easy for him then to let
the external reality set him right and he therefore allows
himself to be influenced by his own interests, his own sympathies and antipathies.

If we aspire to penetrate into the spiritual world, it is all-
important for us to learn to confront our own self with the
same absence of bias with which we confront the external
world. In the ancient Pythagorean schools this truth was
formulated in strictly precise terms, particularly for the
department of knowledge concerned with the question of
immortality. Think of all the people who are interested in
the subject of immortality. It is normal for men to long for
immortality, for a life beyond birth and death. But that is a
purely personal interest, a personal longing. You will not be
particularly interested if a tumbler gets broken; but if people
had the same personal interest in the continued existence of a
tumbler, even if broken, as they have in the immortality of
the soul, you may be sure that most of them would believe in
the immortality of a tumbler!

For this reason it was felt in the Pythagorean schools that
no-one is really ready to know the truth about immortality
unless he could endure it if he were told that man is not
immortal and his question whether man is immortal had to
be answered with a 'no'. If immortality is to mean anything
for a man himself in the spiritual world, then—so said the
teacher in the Pythagorean schools—he must not yearn for it;
for as long as a man yearns for immortality, what he says
about it will not be objective. Weighty opinions about the
life beyond birth and death can come only from those who
could contemplate the grave with equal calm if there were no
immortality. This was the teaching in the Pythagorean
schools because it was essential that the pupils should understand how difficult it is to be mature enough to face the
truth.

To state a truth on the basis of this maturity calls for very special preparation, which requires us to be entirely uninterested in its implications. Especially with regard to immortality, more than other problems, it is quite impossible to think that many people have no interest in the subject. Of course there are people who have been told about reincarnation and the eternity of man's existence, in spite of the fact that they are by no means disinterested. Everyone can take in the truth and use it for the benefit of life—including those who have not the task of formulating it themselves. There is no reason to reject a truth because one does not feel ready for it. On the contrary, it is quite sufficient for the needs of life to receive the truth and dedicate one's powers to its service.

What is the necessary complement to the reception of truths? They can be received and assimilated without misgiving even if we are not completely ready for them. But the necessary complement is this.—To make ourselves ready for truth with the same ardour with which we long for it in order to have inner peace, contentment and a sure footing in life, and at the same time to be cautious in proclaiming higher truths ourselves—truths which can only be confirmed in the spiritual world.

An important precept for our spiritual life can be gained from this. We should be receptive to anything we need and apply it in life; but we should be duly suspicious of truths we ourselves proclaim, especially if they are connected with our own astral experiences. This means that we must be particularly careful about making use of astral experiences at points where we cannot be disinterested, especially at the point where our own life comes into consideration.

Let us assume that through his astral development a man is mature enough to ascertain something that will be his destiny tomorrow. That is a personal experience. He should, however, refrain from making investigations in the book of his personal life for there he cannot possibly be disinterested. People may ask why it is that clairvoyants do not try to ascertain the time of their own death. The reason is that they could never be wholly disinterested about such a happening and they must hold aloof from everything relating to their personal concerns. We can only investigate in the spiritual worlds, with any hope that the results will have objective validity, matters which we are quite sure are unrelated to our personal concerns. A man who resolves to promulgate only what is objectively valid, apart altogether from his own interests, must never speak about anything that concerns or affects himself as the result of investigations or impressions from a higher world. He must be quite certain that his personal interests have played no part whatever in these results. But it is extremely difficult for him to be quite sure of this.

It is therefore a fundamental principle at the beginning of all spiritual aspirations that efforts should be made not to regard as authoritative anything that affects one personally. Everything personal must be strictly excluded. I need only add that this is extremely difficult to do: often enough when one thinks that everything of a personal nature has been excluded it proves not to have been so. For this reason, most of the astral pictures which appear to people are nothing more than a kind of reflection of their own wishes and passions. These spiritual experiences do no harm at all as long as people are strong-minded enough to remind themselves that they must be suspicious of them. Only when that strength of mind fails, when a man comes to regard these experiences as authoritative in his life—only then does he lose his bearings. It is then rather as if he were trying to get out of a room at a place where there is no door and consequently he runs his head against the wall. Hence this principle must never be forgotten: *Test your spiritual experiences with extreme caution.* No other value save that of being a means of knowledge, of enlightenment, should attach to these experiences; our personal life should not be governed or directed by them. If they are regarded as means of enlightenment then we are on safe ground, for in that case, as soon as a contradictory idea crops up it can also be corrected.

What I have said today is only part of the many studies we shall undertake this winter. I also wanted to give you something that can be a preparation for the study of Psychosophy, of man's life of soul, which will be the subject of the lectures during the week following the General Meeting.

THE TASKS OF THE FIFTH POST-ATLANTEAN EPOCH

We have often studied the period of evolution following the Atlantean catastrophe and the epochs of post-Atlantean civilisation: the Old Indian, Old Persian, Egypto-Chaldean, Graeco-Roman, and now the fifth, in which we ourselves are living. There will be two more epochs, making seven in all, before there is another great catastrophe.

The accounts given have naturally been of different aspects of these culture-epochs, for an idea of the future can be formed only by knowing how we are related to each of them. I have often said that there is a correspondence between the individual human being as a 'Microcosm', a 'little world', and the 'Macrocosm', the 'great world'. Man, the 'little world', is in every respect a replica, a copy, of the 'great world'. This is literally true, but stated in this form it is a very abstract truth and does not lead us very far. It becomes significant only if we can go on and show in detail how the individual human being is to be conceived as a Microcosm compared with the Macrocosm.

The man of to-day belongs to all the seven post-Atlantean epochs for he has been, or will be, incarnated in each of them. In every incarnation we receive what that particular epoch can give us. Thus we bear within ourselves the fruits of past phases of evolution. Our intrinsic qualities and talents are those we have acquired during the several post-Atlantean epochs and they lie more or less within the range of human consciousness as it is to-day. On the other hand, during our Atlantean incarnations there were very different states of consciousness and what we then acquired has, generally speaking, been pressed down into the subconscious. It does not therefore reverberate within us as strongly as what was acquired in later incarnations during the post-Atlantean epoch. In the much earlier Atlantean epoch human consciousness was by no means as wideawake as it became later on and men were not then able to the same extent to injure their own development. Consequently the fruits of Atlantean evolution within us are more in harmony with the World-Order than has been the case since we have been able ourselves to create disorder in our own being. Ahrimanic and Luciferic influences were active during the Atlantean epoch too, but the effect of them upon man was altogether different. Nor was man then in a position to protect himself against them.

The ever-increasing development of human consciousness is the essential feature of post-Atlantean civilisation. The evolution of mankind in the period between the catastrophe which overwhelmed Atlantis and the one that will bring the post-Atlantean epoch to an end may be thought of as a macrocosmic process; humanity as a whole evolves as one great being through the seven post-Atlantean epochs. And the most important phases in the evolution of consciousness during these seven epochs resemble what the individual himself undergoes in the seven 'ages' or periods of his own life.

In my book *Occult Science*, and elsewhere, these different life-periods have often been described. The first period covers the seven years from birth to the change of teeth. During this period the physical body of the human being acquires its basic forms and with the coming of the second teeth these forms are to all intents and purposes established. Naturally, the child continues to grow; but speaking generally, the lines of the bodily structures have already been established. What is accomplished in the first seven years is the construction of the bodily *form*. We must be prepared to find these rhythms manifesting in us in a wide variety of ways. For instance, there is a difference between the first teeth, which appear during the earliest years of life and then fall out, to be replaced by the second teeth. The two sets of teeth are the result of essentially different conditions. The first teeth are the inherited product of the organisms of the child's forefathers. The second teeth are the product of the child's own physical constitution. This must be kept firmly in mind. Only by being attentive to such details can the distinction be fully understood. Our first teeth, together with our whole organism, are passed on to us by our forefathers; our second teeth are the product of our own physical organism. In the first case the teeth are a direct inheritance: in the second it is the physical organism that is inherited and this in its turn produces the second teeth.

The second life-period is from the time of the change of teeth to puberty, at about the fourteenth or fifteenth year. The important process now is the development of the etheric body. The third period, to about the twenty-first year, covers the development of the astral body. Then follows the development of the Ego, with the progressive development of the Sentient Soul, the Intellectual or Mind-Soul and the Spiritual Soul (Consciousness-Soul).

These are the different periods in man's life: but as you certainly know, the first period of seven years alone follows a completely regular pattern, and this is as it should be for man of the present age. The regularity apparent in the first three life-periods is not found in the later ones, nor can their length be defined with exactitude. If we ask why this is so, the answer is that in world-evolution which proceeds in rhythms of seven periods, the fourth plays a middle part. Thus in the post-Atlantean era we already have within us the fruits of the first four epochs; we are now living in the fifth and moving towards the sixth.

There is undoubtedly a certain correspondence between the evolution of the post-Atlantean epochs and that of the individual human being. Here again there is evidence of correspondence between the macrocosmic and the microcosmic.

Let us consider what was particularly characteristic of the

first post-Atlantean epoch. We call it the Old Indian epoch because the character of post-Atlantean evolution in general was especially marked in the people of India. In this epoch there existed a sublime, all-embracing wisdom, with wide ramifications. In principle, the teachings given by the seven holy Rishis were identical with what was actually seen in the spiritual world by natural clairvoyants and also by very many of the people of that time. This ancient knowledge was present in the Old Indian epoch as a heritage from still earlier times. In the Atlantean epoch it had been experienced clairvoyantly, but it had now become more of an inherited, primal wisdom, preserved and made known by those who, like the Rishis, had risen through Initiation to the spiritual worlds. Basically, all the wisdom that penetrated into human consciousness was inherited and therefore essentially different from our modern knowledge.

It would be quite wrong to attempt to express the sublime truths proclaimed by the holy Rishis in the first post-Atlantean epoch in terms such as those used in modern scholarship; moreover it would hardly be possible to do so, because the forms assumed by scholarship as it is to-day appeared only in the course of post-Atlantean culture. The knowledge possessed by the ancient Rishis was of a very different character. Anyone capable of proclaiming it felt it working and seething within him, rising up spontaneously. To understand what knowledge was in those days we must realise above all that it did not in any way rely upon memory. Please keep this very specially in mind. Memory is the most important factor when knowledge is being transmitted to-day. A professor or a public speaker must take care that he knows beforehand what he is going to say from the rostrum, and then draw it out of his memory. True, there are people who deny that they do any such thing, insisting that they simply follow their own genius. But they don't affect the argument. The communication of knowledge to-day depends almost entirely upon memory.

Things were very different in the Old Indian epoch. It

would be true to say that knowledge arose at the actual moment of speaking. In those early times knowledge was not prepared beforehand as it so often is to-day. The ancient Rishi did not prepare what he had to say and then memorise it. The preparation he made was to induce in himself a mood of piety, of reverence. It was his mood and his feelings that he prepared, not the content of what he was about to communicate. And then, while it was being communicated it was as if he were reading from an invisible script. It would have been unthinkable in those days for listeners to take down in writing what was being said; anything recorded in this way would have been considered quite worthless. Value was attached only to what a man preserved in his soul and might later reproduce for others. It would have been regarded as desecration to write anything down. The view rightly held at that time was that what is transcribed is not, and cannot be, the same as the oral communication.

This way of thinking persisted for a very long time. Such matters are retained in the feelings much longer than in the intellect and when, in the Middle Ages, the art of printing was added to that of writing, it was at first regarded as black magic. Old feelings were still astir in men and they felt that what is meant to pass directly from soul to soul should not be preserved in the grotesque form of letters and words printed on sheets of white paper. People were convinced that this transformed the knowledge to be communicated into something lifeless which might, moreover, subsequently be revived with anything but beneficial results. The direct streaming of knowledge from soul to soul was characteristic of the times we are considering. It was a prominent feature in the cultural life of the first post-Atlantean epoch and must be recognised if we are to understand, for instance, how it came about that Greek and even old Germanic rhapsodists could go from place to place reciting their very lengthy poems. This would never have been possible if they had been obliged to rely upon memory. It was a power and a quality of soul much more alive than memory that lay behind their recitations. Nowadays if we are to recite a poem we must have learnt it beforehand; but what those men were reciting was an actual experience in them, a kind of new creation. Moreover a direct expression of the life of soul was then more clearly in evidence than it is now, when—with some justification in view of prevailing conditions—it is apt to be suppressed. What is considered of main importance nowadays in recitation is the actual meaning of the words. It was not so, even in the Middle Ages, when a minstrel was reciting the *Niebelungenlied*, for instance. He still had a feeling for the inner rhythm and would stamp his feet to mark the rise and fall of the verse as he strode forward and back. But this was only an aftermath of what had been customary in more ancient times. You would have an erroneous idea of the Rishis and their pupils if you were to think that they had not faithfully communicated the old Atlantean knowledge. Even if the pupils in our schools were to fill their exercise books from cover to cover, they would not have reproduced what had been said as faithfully as the Indian Rishis reproduced the ancient wisdom.

The characteristic feature of the epochs which followed was that the flow of Atlantean knowledge came to a standstill. Until the decline of the Old Indian culture-epoch, knowledge received by men in the form of an inheritance continually increased. In essentials, however, the increase ceased with the close of this epoch: thereafter, hardly anything new could be produced from existing knowledge. An increase of knowledge was therefore possible only in the first epoch; thereafter it ceased. In the Old Persian epoch, among men influenced by Zoroastrianism, something began in connection with knowledge of the external world which can be compared with the second period in human life and is, in fact, best understood through such a comparison. In a spiritual respect the Old Indian culture-epoch is comparable with the first period in human life, from birth to the seventh year. During this period the basic forms are developed; whatever comes later is merely expansion within these

established forms. What followed in the Old Persian epoch
can similarly be compared with a kind of school-learning,
the kind of learning connected with the second life-period.
Only we must be clear who were the pupils and who were
the teachers. At this point there is something I want to
interpolate.

You must have been struck by the difference between the
figure of Zarathustra, the Leader of the second post-
Atlantean epoch, and the Indian Rishis. Whereas the Rishis
seem to be consecrated individuals stemming from a primor-
dial past, to be vessels into whom old Atlantean wisdom has
poured, Zarathustra appears as the first historical personality to be initiated into a genuinely post-Atlantean Mystery-
knowledge, that is to say, knowledge presented in such a way
that it could be understood only by the intelligence of post-
Atlantean humanity. Something new has therefore made its
appearance. True, during the early period it was preeminently supersensible knowledge that was acquired in the
Zoroastrian schools. Nevertheless it was there that knowledge
began for the first time to take the form of concepts. The
ancient knowledge possessed by the Rishis cannot be reproduced in the forms of modern scholarship but to some extent
this *is* possible with the Zoroastrian knowledge. This is
knowledge of an altogether supersensible character and
concerned entirely with the supersensible world but it is
clothed in concepts comparable with those current during
the post-Atlantean epoch in general. Among the followers of
Zarathustra a systematic development of concepts took
place. To sum up: The treasure-store of ancient wisdom
which had evolved until the end of the Old Indian epoch and
continued from generation to generation, was accepted.
Nothing new was added but the old was elaborated. A comparison, for example, with the production nowadays of a
book on occultism will help us to picture the task of the
Mysteries of the second post-Atlantean epoch. The contents
of any book resulting from genuine investigations into the
higher worlds could of course be presented as an entirely

logical exposition in the physical world. This might be done. But in that case my book *Occult Science*, for example, would have to consist of fifty volumes at least, each of them as bulky as the present one. There is, however, another way of doing things, namely to leave something to the reader, to induce the reader to think things out for himself. That is what must be attempted nowadays, for otherwise no progress in occultism could be made. To-day, in the fifth post-Atlantean epoch, with the intellectual concepts developed by humanity, it is possible to approach and also to assimilate occult knowledge. But in Zarathustra's time the concepts in which to clothe occult facts had first to be discovered and gradually elaborated. There were then no branches of knowledge such as exist to-day. Something capable of being clothed in human concepts had survived from the time of the ancient Rishis, but the concepts as such had to be formulated before the supersensible facts could be clothed in them. It was then, for the first time, that man-made concepts were used to grasp supersensible realities. The Rishis had spoken in the only way in which, in their day, supersensible knowledge could be communicated. They poured their knowledge from soul to soul in an unceasing flow of pictures. They were unconcerned with cause and effect, with concepts and categories such as are familiar to us to-day. This was a much later development. In the field of supersensible knowledge a beginning was made in the second post-Atlantean epoch. It was then that man first became aware of the opposition offered by material existence and therewith the need to express supersensible facts in forms of thought employed on the physical plane. This was the basic task of the second post-Atlantean epoch.

By the third epoch, that of Egypto-Chaldean culture, concepts of supersensible realities were actually in existence. This again is difficult for the modern mind to grasp. There was no physical science but there were concepts of supersensible facts and happenings which had been acquired in a supersensible way, and these concepts could be expressed in forms of thought applicable to the physical plane. In the third post-Atlantean epoch men began to apply to the physical world itself what they had learnt from the supersensible world. This again can be compared with the third period in the life of a human being. In the second period he learns without proceeding to apply what he has learnt. In the third life-period most human beings have to apply their knowledge to the physical plane. The pupils of Zarathustra in the second culture-epoch were pupils of heavenly knowledge; now men began to apply to the physical plane what they had learnt. It may help us to picture this if we say that through their visions men learnt that the supersensible can be expressed by a triangle—a triangle taken as an image of the supersensible; that the supersensible nature of man, permeating the physical, can be conceived as threefold. Other concepts too were mastered, enabling physical things to be related to supersensible facts. Geometry, for instance, was first mastered in the form of symbolic concepts. In short, concepts were now available and were applied by the Egyptians to the art of land-surveying, also to agriculture, and by the Chaldeans in their study of the stars and in the founding of Astrology and Astronomy. What had previously been regarded as purely supersensible was now applied to things physically seen. In the third culture-epoch, then, men began for the first time to apply supersensible knowledge to the phenomena of the world of sense.

In the fourth epoch, the Graeco-Latin, it was especially important that men should come to see that what they were doing was to apply to the physical plane knowledge derived from supersensible sources. Hitherto they had acted without questioning whether this was actually the case. The ancient Rishis had no need for such questioning because the knowledge streamed into them directly from the spiritual world. In the epoch of Zarathustra men assimilated the supersensible knowledge and were fully aware how it originated. In the Egypto-Chaldean epoch men invested the concepts derived from the supersensible world with knowledge they had acquired in the physical world. And in the fourth epoch (the Graeco-Latin) they began to ask whether it is right to apply to the physical world what has come from the spiritual world. Is what has been spiritually acquired in fact applicable to physical things?—Men could not put this to themselves as a definite question until the fourth culture-epoch, after they had for some time been applying supersensible knowledge in all naivety to physical experiences and observations. Now they became conscientious in regard to their own doings and began to ask whether it is justifiable to apply supersensible concepts to physical facts.

Now when any epoch has an important task to perform, it always happens that some individual is particularly alive to its nature and responsible for fulfilling it. In this case, such an individual would have been struck by the thought as to whether one has the right to apply supersensible concepts to physical facts. Can anyone really predict how things will develop? It is obvious that *Plato*, for example, had a living connection with the ancient world and still applied concepts in their old form to the physical world. It was his pupil *Aristotle* who asked whether it is right to do this.—And so Aristotle became the founder of Logic.

People who reject Spiritual Science should just ask themselves why man had managed to get on without any system of Logic. Had they never before the fourth epoch felt any need for it?—To a clear-sighted view of evolution, important periods occur at definite points of time. One such period lies between Plato and Aristotle. Here we have before us a situation that is related in a certain way to the connection with the spiritual world existing in the Atlantean epoch. True, the living spiritual knowledge died out with the Old Indian culture-epoch, but something new had nevertheless been brought down to the physical plane. Now, in this later age, man had begun to develop a critical faculty, and to ask how ideas about supersensible reality may be applied to physical things. This is a sign that man only now became conscious that he himself achieves something when he is observing the external world, that he is actually bringing something down into the sense-world. This was a significant state of things.

We can still feel that concepts and ideas are in essence supersensible when we regard their very character as being a guarantee for the existence of the supersensible world. But only few feel this. What concepts and ideas contain is for most people extremely tenuous. And although there is something in them which can provide complete proof of man's immortality, it would be impossible to convince him, because compared with the solid, material reality for which he longs, concepts and ideas are as unsubstantial as a cobweb. They are, in fact, the last and slenderest thread spun by man out of the spiritual world since his descent into the physical world. And at the very time when he had left the spiritual world altogether and remained linked to it by this last, slender thread only—a thread in which he no longer had any faith—there came the mightiest incision from the supersensible world: the Christ Impulse. The greatest of all spiritual realities appeared in our post-Atlantean epoch at a time when man was least able to recognise the supersensible, because the only spiritual quality remaining to him was his feeling for concepts and ideas.

For anyone studying the evolution of humanity as a whole it would be interesting in a strictly scientific sense—apart from the tornado-like effect it may have on the soul—to set side by side the infinite spirituality of the Christ Being who entered into humanity and the fact that shortly before His coming man had been wondering how far the last thread of spirituality within him was connected with the supersensible world—in other words, to contrast the Christ Principle with Aristotelian Logic, that web of wholly abstract concepts and ideas. No greater disparity can be imagined than that between the spirituality which came down to the physical plane in the Being of Christ and the spirituality which man had preserved for himself. You will therefore understand that with the web of concepts available in Aristotelianism it was simply not possible in the first centuries of Christendom to comprehend the spiritual nature of Christ. And then, gradually, efforts were made to grasp the facts of world-history and the evolution of humanity in such a way that Aristotelian Logic could be applied. This was the task facing medieval philosophy.

It is significant that the fourth post-Atlantean epoch may be compared with the period of Ego-development in man's life. It was in this epoch that the 'I' of humanity itself streamed into evolution, at the time when man was further removed from the spiritual world than he had ever been and was therefore at first quite incapable of accepting Christ except through faith. Christianity was bound at first to be a matter of faith and is only now beginning, very gradually, to be a matter of knowledge. We have only just begun to bring the light of spiritual knowledge to bear upon the Gospels. For hundreds upon hundreds of years Christianity could only be a matter of faith, because man had reached the lowest point of his descent from the spiritual worlds.

This was the situation in the fourth post-Atlantean epoch. But after the lowest point the re-ascent must begin. Although in a certain respect this epoch brought man to the lowest point of descent, it also gave him the strongest spiritual impulse upwards. Naturally, this was beyond his comprehension then and will be understood only in the epochs still to come. We can, however, recognise the task before us: it is *to permeate our concepts and ideas with spirituality*.

World-evolution is not a simple, straightforward process. When a ball begins to roll in a certain direction, inertia will keep it rolling unless its course is changed by some other impact. Similarly, pre-Christian culture tended to preserve and maintain the downward plunge into the physical world until our own time. The upward urge is only just beginning and periodically needs a new impetus.

The downward tendency is particularly evident in the way men think, even in a great deal of what is called Philosophy to-day. Aristotle still recognised that spiritual reality is within the grasp of human concepts. But a few centuries after him men were no longer able to understand how the activity of the human mind can make contact with reality. The most arid, most barren element in the development of the old mode of thinking is represented by Kantianism and everything related to it. For Kant's philosophy severs all connection between the concepts a man evolves, between ideas as inner experiences, and what concepts and ideas are in reality. Kantianism is in the process of withering away and has no living impulse to give to the future. It will now no longer surprise you that the conclusion of my lectures on Psychosophy had a theosophical background. I have made it clear that in all our activities, and especially in connection with knowledge of the soul, our task is to take the knowledge bestowed by the gods on men in earlier days and brought down as a stimulus to our thought, and offer it up again at the altars of the gods. But the ideas and concepts we make our own must have their origin in spirituality.

Psychology as a science must be cultivated in such a way that it can emerge from the decadence into which it has fallen. This is not said out of arrogance but because it is what the times demand. There have been and there still are many psychologists: but they all work with concepts totally devoid of spirituality. It is significant that in 1874 a man like *Franz Brentano* published only the first volume of his *Psychology*, which in spite of certain distortions, is generally sound. He had announced the second volume for publication in the same year; but he came to a standstill and could not finish it. He was able to give an outline of what the content was to have been but to get beyond that a spiritual impulse would have been needed.

Modern psychologies, for example those written by *Wundt* and *Lipps*, do not really deserve the name because they work only with ideas previously evolved and it was obvious from the outset that nothing would come of them. Brentano's *Psychology* might have led to something but he came to a standstill—which is the fate of all dying sciences. It will not happen so quickly in the case of the natural sciences, where cut-and-dried concepts can be applied because facts are being collected and may be allowed to speak for themselves. With Psychology—the science of the soul—this is much less practicable, for the whole foundation disappears if any attempt is made to work with the ordinary, rigid concepts. You don't immediately lose touch with a heart-muscle even if you analyse it as if it were a mineral product and have no knowledge of its real nature. But you cannot analyse the soul in the same way.

The sciences are as it were dying from above downwards. And it will gradually dawn on men that while they are certainly able to turn the laws of nature to account, this is something quite independent of science itself. To construct machines and instruments, telephones and the like, is a very different matter from a basic understanding of the sciences, let alone the ability to further their progress. A man may have no fundamental understanding of electricity and yet be able to construct electrical apparatus. Science in the real sense is, however, gradually declining and we have now reached a point where in its present form it must be given new life through spiritual science. In our fifth culture-epoch science is rolling downwards by its own momentum: when the ball can roll no further it will come to a standstill, as Brentano did. At this time, therefore, it is imperative that the ascent of humanity should be given a stronger and stronger stimulus. This will indeed take place, but only if efforts continue to be made to fertilise knowledge acquired from outside with what spiritual investigation has to offer.

As I have said before, a kind of repetition of the old Egypto-Chaldean epoch will become apparent during our own fifth epoch. This repetition is at present only just beginning. Indications of this might have become clear to you during this General Meeting. Think, for instance, of Herr Seiler's lecture on Astrology. You will have felt that as students of Spiritual Science you are able to apply to astrological concepts ideas which would be quite impossible for a conventional astronomer, who will inevitably treat anything connected with Astrology as nonsense. This has nothing to do with the intrinsic character of Astronomy. As a matter of fact, Astronomy is the science *par excellence* which lends itself readily to being led back again to spirituality; from what Astronomy has at present to offer it would be easy to pass to the basic truths of Astrology which is so often derided. What stands in the way is that the general attitude of mind is so far removed from any return to spirituality. It will take time to build the bridge between Astronomy and Astrology and meanwhile all sorts of theories will be devised in an attempt to give a purely materialistic explanation of the planetary movements, and so on. In the case of the chemical and biological sciences the bridge will be even more difficult to build.

The building of a bridge can be easiest of all in the domain of Psychology—the science of the soul. The first requisite will be to understand the conclusion of my lectures on 'Psychosophy' where I showed that the stream of soul-life flows not only from the past into the future but also from the future into the past. *There are two streams of time: the etheric stream, flowing into the future, and the astral stream, moving from the future back into the past.* It is unlikely that anyone in the world today will discover anything of this character without a spiritual impulse, but there can be no real grasp of the life of soul until we recognise that something is perpetually coming towards us from the future. This concept is essential. We shall have to rid ourselves of the mode of thought which looks only to the past when cause and effect are being considered. We shall have to learn to speak of the future as something real, something moving towards us, just as we trail the past behind us. It will be a long time before such concepts are accepted; but until they are there will be no real Psychology.

The nineteenth century produced a really bright idea: Psychology without Soul! People were very proud of it.

Roughly, what it meant was that psychological study should be confined to the external manifestations of the human soul and should take no account of the soul itself from which they originated. A science of the soul without soul! As a method this might be possible; but the outcome, to use a rough analogy, is a meal without food. That is modern Psychology. People are anything but satisfied if you give them a meal with nothing on their plates, but nineteenth century science was wonderfully content with a Psychology without soul. Such a trend began at a comparatively early stage and spiritual life must flow as a strong impulse into this whole domain.

The old life has come to an end and a new life must begin. We must feel that there was given to us from the ancient Atlantean epoch a primeval wisdom which has gradually withered away and that in our present incarnation we are faced with the task of gathering a new wisdom for the men of a later time. To make this possible was the purpose of the Christ Impulse, and the activity and power of that Impulse will continually increase. It may be that the Christ Impulse will work most strongly when all tradition—in history too— has died away and men find their way to Christ Himself as the true reality.

You can see, then, that the course of post-Atlantean evolution and the life of an individual human being are comparable as Macrocosm with Microcosm. But the individual is in a strange situation. What is there left to him in the second part of his life but to absorb and assimilate what he acquired for himself in the first half? And when that is all used up, death follows. The spirit alone can be victorious over death and carry forward into a new incarnation what begins to decay after the half-way point of life has been passed. Development is on the ascent until the thirty-fifth year. After that there is decline. But it is precisely then that the spirit takes a hand. What it cannot incorporate into the bodily nature of man during the second half of life it brings to blossom in a later incarnation. As the body withers the spirit gradually comes to fruition.

The macrocosm of humanity as a whole reveals a similar picture. Until the fourth post-Atlantean epoch there is a youthful, thriving development of culture. From then onwards there is a decline—symptoms of death everywhere in the evolution of human consciousness, but at the same time the inflow of new spiritual life which will incarnate again as the spiritual life of humanity in the culture-epoch following our own. But man must work with full consciousness on what is subsequently to incarnate again. The rest will die away. We can look prophetically into the future and see the birth of many sciences seeming to benefit post-Atlantean civilisation although they belong to what is dying. But the life that is poured into humanity under the direct influence of the Christ Impulse will come to manifestation in the future just as the Atlantean knowledge came again to manifestation in the holy Rishis.

Ordinary science knows of the Copernican system only that part which is in process of dying. The part that will live on and bear fruit—and that is not the part that has been influential for four centuries—must now be mastered by men through their own efforts. Copernicanism as presented to-day is not strictly true. Spiritual investigation alone can reveal its real truth. The same holds good for Astronomy, and for everything else that is regarded as knowledge to-day. Science can of course be of practical use and as technology completely justified. But in so far as it pretends to contribute to human knowledge in its real form, it is a dead product. It is useful for the immediate handiwork of men and for that no spiritual content is necessary. But as far as it purports to have anything vital to say about the mysteries of the Universe it belongs to the culture that is dying. If knowledge of the mysteries of the Universe is to be enriched, the orthodox science of to-day must be imbued with life through the findings of Spiritual Science.

The foregoing lectures were intended as an introduction to the study of St. Mark's Gospel which we shall now begin. I had first to show how essential this greatest of all spiritual impulses was for human evolution just at the time when only the last, most tenuous threads of spirituality remained to mankind.

THE SYMBOLIC LANGUAGE OF THE MACROCOSM IN THE GOSPEL OF ST. MARK

My book *Christianity as Mystical Fact* will have made it clear to all of you that if the Gospels are to be rightly understood, they must be regarded as treatises of Initiation. This means that in essence they are adaptations of rites and rituals of Initiation. Scripts of this nature indicated the path along which the candidate was led step by step to the higher worlds, how he must undergo certain experiences and awaken forces slumbering in his soul, how each higher stage was related to the one below, until at the stage of Initiation itself the spiritual world penetrated into his soul and revealed its mysteries. At this stage he gazed into the spiritual worlds and a vista of the Beings of the Hierarchies lay open before him. The content of these Initiation-scripts, then, was a description of the experiences which every candidate for Initiation had to undergo.

In pre-Christian times many human beings were initiated in the different centres of the Mysteries. Generally speaking the process was the same, although there were variations in details. The candidates were led stage by stage to the point where they were able to gaze into the spiritual world and the Beings of the Hierarchies were before them as spiritual—not physical—realities. That is what happened in pre-Christian times. But what did Christianity, what did the Christ Impulse

---

* At the beginning of this lecture Dr. Steiner emphasised that those relatively new to the study of Spiritual Science would find many things difficult to understand. He added that unless the necessary efforts were made by these recent Members to master the elementary principles of Spiritual Science, erroneous ideas would be inevitable.

signify for those who had been initiated in the ancient Mysteries? It signified that a Being, known in the physical world as Jesus of Nazareth, had revealed the secrets of the spiritual world in a new way, not in the way that had been customary in the pre-Christian Mysteries. A man who had been initiated according to the ancient rites was able to speak to others about the secrets of the spiritual worlds. But the Christ Event meant that something had come to pass whereby without having traversed the usual paths, Jesus of Nazareth was able to speak of these secrets through what happened at the Baptism in Jordan, when the Christ Being entered into him. From the moment when in an event of supreme historical significance, Jesus of Nazareth was thus initiated, the Christ Spirit spoke to those around Him of the secrets of the spiritual worlds. Christ made manifest on the physical plane, for all the world to see, something that in former times could be attained only in the secrecy of the Mysteries by those who were to be initiated: they could then go forth and speak to their fellow-men of the secrets of the spiritual worlds. We can imagine ourselves looking into sanctuaries of the ancient Mysteries and seeing how the aspirants were initiated by the Hierophants and were then able to look into the spiritual worlds and go forth to teach of them. All the rites of Initiation took place in the deepest secrecy of the temples; and outside the Mysteries there was no possibility of speaking at first hand about the spiritual worlds. But now, what had been enacted time and time again in the secrecy of the Mysteries was brought into the open in Palestine, presented there as an historical event, as the story of Jesus of Nazareth, which culminated in an Initiation of supreme significance in world-history. This was the Mystery of Golgotha. The supreme Mystery enacted as an historic fact before the eyes of all the world—this is how we must picture the connection of the Mystery of Golgotha with the Mysteries of pre-Christian times.

Now the directives for Initiation, although concerned in essentials with the same stages, differed in details among the peoples living in different parts of the Earth and these directives were adapted to the nature of the individuals living in different places at different times. Let us think of the soul of one of those generally called the Evangelists who participated in the writing of our Gospels. From their own occult training such men had some knowledge of the directives for Initiation among various peoples and in various Mysteries. They knew what experiences a man must undergo before he could proclaim the secrets of the spiritual worlds and of the Hierarchies. And now, through the events in Palestine and the Mystery of Golgotha, they had been made aware that what could previously be witnessed only by those who had attained Initiation in the Mysteries, had taken place openly on the stage of world-history and would enter more and more deeply into the hearts and souls of all men.

The Evangelists were not biographers in our sense of the word. They did not include in their writings details of no significance to the world which it is quite unnecessary for anyone to know. They were not the kind of biographers who ferret out every detail of a man's private affairs. They described the life of Christ by saying that in Jesus of Nazareth, in whom the Christ was present, something happened which had been witnessed again and again in the Mysteries but never as an historic event, concentrated into a few years. It was now an historic reality, yet it was a repetition of the temple-rituals.—The life of Jesus could therefore have been described by specifying the stages passed through in other circumstances during the process of Initiation.

The directives for Initiation in the ancient Mysteries are found again in the Gospels and indications are given there of the reason why what had formerly taken place in the deep secrecy of the temples had now been transferred to the great arena of world-history. And it is the writer of St. Mark's Gospel who, at the outset, states why he is in a position to write of an historic event which in fact fulfils a rule of Initiation though enacted on an infinitely greater scale. From the beginning he speaks of how humanity has developed in such a way that this great event might come to pass and Initiation might be transferred from the secrecy of the temple-sanctuaries to the arena of history. He proclaims that this is connected with an event foretold by the Hebrew prophets. For the Mystery of Golgotha had been foreseen and foretold by the true Initiates, among whom the Hebrew prophets may, in a certain sense, be included.

If we try to penetrate into the soul of a man such as the prophet Isaiah, the meaning of the words at the beginning of St. Mark's Gospel is approximately this: that a time will come when the souls of men will not be as they are at present. This time is already now being prepared for.—This was Isaiah's view in his own day. What did he really mean? The deeply impressive words of this prophet with which St. Mark's Gospel begins, are, as you know, usually rendered:

'Behold, I send my messenger before thy face which shall prepare thy way before thee. The voice of one crying in the wilderness. Prepare ye the way of the Lord, make his paths straight.'*

In these words the prophet Isaiah points to the greatest event in all world-history—the Mystery of Golgotha in Palestine. You know what trouble we have had when studying the other Gospels to make the most important passages to some extent intelligible in translation. What really matters is to render the turns of phrases in a way that will convey the profound meaning of the original language. The words should not merely lend themselves to theoretical interpretation but be able to arouse feelings similar to those aroused in men who understood the inherent character of the language in current use. Language at that time was not as abstract, dry and prosaic as it has now become. Its character as the means of verbal expression was such that in addition to the usual meaning of the words spoken the hearer was always aware of a richer significance and fullness of content and knew precisely what that content indicated. At that time a whole world of meaning was heard in the words.

* Dr. Steiner quoted the translation by Carl Weizsäcker.

The ancient Hebrew language was particularly rich in this
respect, even when the picture used was drawn from the
realm of the senses. Phrases such as 'prepare the way' or
'make his paths straight' are pictures derived entirely from
the sense-world—as if a way, or a path, were being prepared
with spades and shovels. But it was a peculiar feature of
Hebrew—a language of outstanding grandeur among the
others—that behind these expressions which were applied to
outer things, spiritual worlds could be apprehended with
great exactness. Fanciful interpretations were unheard of
and the procedure was unlike that adopted by our modern
scholars when they read all sorts of implications into the
works of poets. Arbitrary interpolations were quite impossible. This was partly because in the ancient Hebrew
language the vowels were not marked in the script, and by
varying them, world-secrets could be revealed in the
sounds themselves. In those days men had a true feeling for
all this.

In Greek—the language of the Gospel texts —this was no
longer the case to the same extent. All the same, far better
renderings than those produced by most translators of the
Gospels would have been possible, even without occult
knowledge. What has happened is that for the most part one
translator has just copied another without any searching
philological study of the passages in the Greek texts. Later
on I will give you definite examples of errors that have been
made. I do not want to interrupt our study to-day and will
try, not on a philological basis but with the help of knowledge derived from spiritual-scientific investigations, to
clarify the most significant passage occurring at the beginning of the Gospel of St. Mark. The following is a prophecy
of Isaiah, showing what the event of Palestine was to mean.

The Greek text is as follows:

'ἰδοὺ ἐγὼ ἀποστέλλω τὸν ἄγγελόν μου πρὸ προσώπου σου, ὃς
κατασκευάσει τὴν ὁδόν σου ἔμπροσθεν σον.

φωνὴ βοῶντος ἐν τῇ ἐρήμῳ: ἐτοιμάσατε τὴν ὁδόν κυρίου, εὐθείας
ποιεῖτε τὰς τρίβους αὐτοῦ.

(*Idou egō apostellō ton angelon mou pro prosōpou sou, hos kataskeuasei tēn hodon sou emprosthen sou,*
Phōnē boōntos en tē erēmū. Hetoimasate tēn hodon Kyriou, eutheiās poieite tās tribous autou.)*

It is essential to realise from the beginning that the word *Angelos* ('angel' or 'messenger') was used in those ancient times only in the sense in which we use it when, in speaking of the Hierarchies, we are referring to the Beings of the hierarchical rank immediately above man. When the words τόν ἀγγελον occur, we must realise that a Being of this rank is meant; otherwise the whole sense of the passage will be lost. Spiritual Science alone can provide the basis for understanding such a passage. But once understood it can be a foundation for what occultism has to say about the Christ-event. What is the fundamental significance of the Christ Impulse? We have expressed it as follows.—Through the Christ Impulse the human soul became conscious for the first time that an Ego, an 'I', was to find a place within it, a self-conscious 'I' through which in the further course of Earth-evolution there must be revealed all the secrets formerly revealed by the astral body through natural clairvoyance.

In the epoch of post-Atlantean culture preceding our own, men were still endowed, to some extent, with faculties of clairvoyance which enabled them to see into the spiritual world. In certain abnormal conditions of soul the secrets of the spiritual world streamed into them and they were able to gaze into the realms of the Hierarchies. Vision of the Hierarchy of the Angels persisted the longest and was the most frequent. The Angels were known as Beings belonging to the rank immediately above man. In the times of ancient clairvoyance men were not aware that they themselves possessed a faculty capable of leading them into the spiritual

* Translation in the Authorised Version. Mark i, 2–3.

'Behold, I send my messenger before thy face, which shall prepare thy way before thee. The voice of one crying in the wilderness, Prepare ye the way of the Lord, make his paths straight.'

worlds; they regarded this possibility as a grace vouchsafed to them from without, as the implanting of spiritual powers in their souls. Hence the Prophets could point to the future, saying: 'The time will come when man will be conscious of his 'I' and know that it is by the self-conscious 'I' that the secrets of the spiritual worlds will be unveiled. Man will be able to say: I penetrate into the secrets of the spiritual world through the power of the 'I' within me.'

But preparation was necessary before this stage could be reached. As the lowest rank of the Hierarchies, man had to be prepared by being sent an example of what he must become. The 'Messenger' or 'Angel' was to proclaim to man that he was to become an 'I' in the full sense of the word. And whereas the mission of earlier Angels had been to reveal the spiritual world, it was now the mission of a particular Angel to carry the revelations to a further stage, to make known to man that he was to enter into full possession of the Ego, the 'I'. The earlier revelations were of a different character, not intended for a self-conscious 'I'.

Isaiah proclaimed that the time of the mystery of the 'I' was to come and that from the host of the Angels one would be deputed to announce this.—Only in this sense can we understand what is meant when it is said that the Angel, the Messenger, was 'sent before'—that is to say, sent before man who was to become a self-conscious 'I'. The one who had been 'sent before' was to come as a Being of the Hierarchy of Angels. No Angel had yet spoken to man as a self-conscious 'I'. So this messenger of whom the prophet Isaiah speaks is to make men aware that they must prepare to make a place in their souls for the 'I', the fully independent 'I'. This passage therefore draws attention to a great revolution in the development of the human soul: whereas hitherto men had always to go out of their bodies in order to reach the spiritual world, henceforward they would be able to remain within their own 'I' and draw forth from the 'I' itself the secrets of that world.

Let us compare a soul of remote antiquity with a soul

living near the time of Christ. When a man of very early pre-Christian centuries strove to rise into the higher worlds he could not retain even the degree of self-consciousness so far developed. He was obliged to discard all consciousness of self and be transported into the world of the Hierarchies, the world of pure spirituality. His consciousness was entirely suppressed.—Such were the conditions in the early pre-Christian era.

What, then, was the situation of a man living in times when in order to enter the spiritual world it was no longer necessary for self-consciousness to be suppressed but when the stage had been reached for the development of the 'I'? Even in the Atlantean epoch the 'I' was already present—in a certain sense; but complete assurance that the greatest secrets and mysteries could flow from the 'I' itself was brought by the Christ Impulse. That is why a man who had achieved the old type of Initiation felt that if he desired to penetrate into the spiritual world and receive its revelations, he must suppress a certain part of his soul and make other parts of it particularly active. The part of his inner being that was gradually to grow into the 'I' had to be suppressed, darkened, to become a desolate waste in the soul. On the other hand the astral body—the body which could make a certain degree of clairvoyance possible—must be fired into activity. And then the old clairvoyant visions lit up within it.

I said that the 'I' was in a certain sense already present, but could not be used to investigate the secrets of the spiritual world. The 'I' had to be suppressed, the astral body fired into activity. But more and more it became impossible to quicken the impulses in the astral body. In olden times one of man's most elementary powers was that he was able to suppress the 'I' and kindle the astral body into activity; the secrets of the spiritual world then streamed into him. But progress in evolution was actually achieved just because the astral body became more and more incapable of receiving the secrets of the spiritual world. Man was obliged to admit to himself that his astral body was becoming more and more incapable of attaining what human beings had once been able to attain with the old faculty of clairvoyance, and the 'I' within him was not strong enough yet to achieve anything itself.

It was the best clairvoyants who were the most strongly aware of something barren, something desolate in the soul. This was the 'I', to which no impulse had yet been given. They were aware, too, how impossible it was to reach the spiritual world through the 'I'. This will give you an idea of the feelings and mood of a man living in the period just before the coming of Christ. Such a man was bound to say to himself that he could no longer unfold in his astral body the powers it once possessed: but as yet he had no alternative impulse, so that there was something barren in his soul, something that could not rise into the spiritual world.

When the time for the Christ Impulse was drawing near, certain methods of training were adopted with the object of acquainting men with that province of the soul which could not yet be filled with the spirit. An individual who aspired to gain entry into the higher worlds was told that he could not rise into those worlds in his astral body, that he must withdraw into that province within him where he would feel as though he had no contact at all with the external world.

This was the mood of soul in an aspirant for Initiation at the time of the Christ Impulse. He said to himself: I must abandon all hope of reaching the spiritual world through the powers of my astral body; the time for that is past and the 'I' is still not ready. But from something within me that is trying to emerge and to penetrate into the spiritual world, I can surmise—no more than surmise—that it is striving with might and main to receive the spiritual impulse.

This experience, known in those days to every seeker for the light of the spirit, was called 'the way into the solitude of the soul', or also, 'the way into the solitude'. The messenger who was to prepare for the Christ-event had therefore to describe the way into the solitude to those who wished to hear about the approaching Impulse. He had himself to know the depths of solitude, to preach from actual experience of the solitude of the soul.

In your study of St. Mark's Gospel you will come to realise more and more clearly that certain lofty spiritual Beings through whom matters of vital importance in human evolution are to take place, look for their instruments in suitable beings of flesh and blood and then descend to live in the soul incarnated in such a body. The messenger of whom Isaiah spoke—who must not be thought of as a man in the ordinary sense—took possession of the soul of the reincarnated Elias—John the Baptist—lived in him and was destined to proclaim to men that the Christ Impulse was at hand.

Where, then, did the voice of this messenger resound? It resounded in what I have just described to you as 'the solitude of the soul'. In St. Mark's Gospel we read: 'Hear the cry in the solitude of the soul'. ἐν τῇ ἐρήμῳ (en tē eremō) must not be translated as if the image of a 'wilderness' were meant in an external sense. ἐν τῇ ἐρήμῳ really means: in the solitude. The imagery used helps us to glimpse the spiritual world.

We shall have a truer understanding of this expression if we devote a little study to the meaning conveyed by another word, *Kyrios*, or Lord, as in the usual rendering of this passage. 'Prepare ye the way of the Lord.' The actual meaning is still discernible in the Greek but can be confirmed by comparison with ancient tradition. In the language of those early times the meaning of a word such as this was not as abstract and shallow as it is to-day. In the age of materialism men have become superficial in their attitude to language and no longer feel as they once did, that words are the bodies of soul-beings, soul-realities, that a whole world lives in the words. The most that can be done to-day is to try to revive something of this feeling, as I have attempted to do in the Mystery Play, *The Portal of Initiation*.

What men felt when they uttered the word *Kyrios* in circumstances such as those indicated, was that it was an image, a picture, of happenings in the inner life of the soul. They felt the 'I' rising upwards from the depths towards the surface of the soul as the appearance of a Lord and Master, the Director and Ruler of the soul-forces. Nowadays we speak of thinking, feeling and willing as servants of the soul. But within the soul there is a Lord, a Kyrios: the 'I' or Ego. In olden times man could not say: 'I think'. He said: 'It thinks'—or, 'it feels, it wills in me.'

At the time when the Lord of the soul-forces, the 'I', appeared as Ruler, the result of this crucial change in the evolution of humanity was that man now said: '*I* think, *I* feel, *I* will.' Hitherto the soul had lived in a certain subconscious state, the captive as it were of its own forces. Now, the Lord of those forces, the 'I', was at hand. This passage in St. Mark's Gospel does not refer to any personality or being but to the emergence of the 'I' as the Lord in the whole structure of the soul. 'The Lord within the soul is at hand.'

This was also made known in the temples where preparation was in train for what was now to take place in mankind. In a mood of holy awe and reverence it was affirmed: Hitherto the soul has had within it only the forces of thinking, feeling and willing—they are its servants: but now the Lord, the Kyrios, is drawing near.—This mighty process will continue to unfold until the end of the Earth-period and its power will constantly increase. The impulse is given by Christ and His life marks the supreme moment in earthly time. The hour on the cosmic clock indicates the point when the 'I' becomes more and more powerful as Lord of the soul-forces. The goal will be attained when the Earth dies in the Cosmos and man rises to higher stages of existence.

Only if you are able to feel what this means can you have an idea of what was prophesied by Isaiah and repeated by John the Baptist. Both of them wished to call attention to the crucial event in the evolution of the human soul. But the word εὐθείας (*eutheiās*) must not be translated 'straight', as is usual; the right rendering is 'open'—that is to say, not only 'straight' but 'open', meaning that the paths along

which the Kyrios comes to the human soul are clear. But
man must himself do something to enable the Kyrios to take
hold of the soul. The way must be made free, must be made
open. In short, if the passage is to be translated at all
intelligibly and at the same time kept fairly close to the
conventional version, it would run somewhat as follows:

'Mark well!'—'behold' is not really correct—'I send my
angel before the 'I' in you; he will prepare the way. Hear the
cry in the solitude of the soul'—the cry for the Lord of the
soul. (The word 'soul' is not actually used but was intui-
tively understood.) 'Prepare the way of the Lord of the soul;
labour to make the path open for him.'

These sentences give an approximate idea of what can be
felt in the words of Isaiah. The Angel in the soul of John the
Baptist used them once again.

What made this possible? To answer this question we shall
have to give some thought to the nature of John the Baptist's
own Initiation and to its effect in his soul.

You know from earlier lectures* that a man can be
initiated either by descending into the depths of his own
soul or by being prepared in such a way that his soul passes
out of the body and its forces pour into the Macrocosm.
Among different peoples these two paths were adopted in
very diverse forms. When a man wished to pour his soul into
the Macrocosm, the twelve stages to be passed were symbolised, so to speak, by the twelve signs of the Zodiac. The
souls flowed out in particular directions, to particular
regions of the Macrocosm. Generally speaking, a very great
deal was achieved, especially for the realisation of some
particular purpose in world-evolution, when a soul had
developed so far that it could receive all the forces originating from the cosmic secrets of a particular zodiacal constellation. The practice in all the ancient rites of Initiation
was that a candidate should be initiated into the secrets of
the Macrocosm in such a way that his soul flowed out in the

* See *Macrocosm and Microcosm*, notably lectures 1 and 3. A
course of eleven lectures given in Vienna, March 1910.

direction, let us say, of Capricorn, or in the case of other candidates, in the directions of Cancer, Libra, Virgo, and so on. I have said repeatedly that there are twelve different possibilities of passing out into the Macrocosm, directions indicated symbolically by the twelve constellations of the Zodiac. If a candidate was unable at once to attain the highest Initiation, the Sun Initiation, but could achieve a partial Initiation only, his soul was directed to the secrets connected with one particular constellation. But his vision must become independent of everything material. This meant that either in the rites of the Mysteries or, as in the case of John the Baptist, by grace from above, the candidate's gaze was guided to a constellation when the Earth lay between him and the constellation—that is to say, by night. Physical eyes see the physical constellation only. But when vision can penetrate through the material Earth— which means that the constellation is masked by the material Earth—then what is seen is not the physical but the *spiritual* reality, that is to say, the secrets which the constellation expresses.

The vision of John the Baptist was trained in such a way that at night he could look through the material Earth into the constellation of Aquarius. When the Angel took possession of his soul he had attained the Aquarius Initiation. Thus John the Baptist was able to place all his faculties and all he knew and felt at the disposal of the Angel, in order that through the Angel the secrets connected with the Aquarius Initiation might be proclaimed and the announcement made of the coming of the 'I', the κύριος, the Lord of the soul-forces.

At the same time, however, the Baptist proclaimed that the time had come when this Aquarius Initiation must be replaced by another, which would make fully intelligible the approaching rulership of the 'I'. Therefore he said to his intimate disciples: I am one who is able to place at the disposal of my Angel all the forces coming from the Aquarius Initiation: but after me must come one whose forces are derived from an even higher source.

If you follow the course of the Sun in the daytime from the constellation of Aries, through Taurus, Gemini and so on, to Virgo, you must follow its progress at night from Libra on to Aquarius and Pisces. This is the direction of the spiritual Sun. John had attained the Aquarius Initiation and announced that He who was to come after him would possess the powers of the Pisces Initiation—the Initiation that followed his own and was regarded as the higher. Hence John the Baptist declared to his disciples: Through the Aquarius Initiation I can place at the disposal of my Angel only those powers which enable him to proclaim the coming of the κύριος the Lord; but there will come One who has the powers symbolised by the Pisces Initiation; and into him the Christ Himself will enter!

With these words John the Baptist pointed to Jesus of Nazareth; and for this reason, tradition assigned to Christ Jesus the symbol of Pisces, the Fishes. Moreover because every outer event is a symbol for inner happenings, fishermen were assigned as helpers of the Pisces Initiate. All these happenings are external, historical events and at the same time profoundly symbolic of the spiritual secrets.

John proclaimed: A higher form of Initiation will be vouchsafed to mankind! He himself could give only the Initiation that comes from Aquarius and he called himself an Aquarian, a Water-man. We must realise more and more clearly that astronomical and cosmic secrets are connected with the images used to express the secrets of Man. John said: 'I have baptised you with water!' Baptism with water lay within the power of those who had received from heaven the Initiation of Aquarius. The spiritual Sun progresses from Aquarius to Pisces (representing the progress from John the Baptist to Jesus of Nazareth) and when a being appeared in the world who had attained the Initiation of the Fishes and was therefore able to receive the spiritual impulse which must be the instrument of the Pisces Initiation—it was then possible for him to baptise, not only as John had baptised, with water, but in the higher sense described by John as 'baptism with the Holy Ghost'.

In this lecture I have put a twofold conception before you. First: the words at the beginning of St. Mark's Gospel indicate processes in the historical evolution of humanity and speak of a higher Power—an Angel who speaks through the body of John the Baptist. Second: the passages in question relate to happenings in the heavens—the progress of the spiritual Sun from the constellation of Aquarius to the constellation of Pisces. Every line of St. Mark's Gospel contains something that can be read rightly only if in following the words we always have in mind both a human and a cosmic-astronomical meaning, and when we realise that there lives in man something that in its true significance can be found only in the heavens.

We must grasp the connection between the secrets of the Macrocosm and the secrets of human nature more exactly than is usual. At the end of this lecture I can do no more than hint at what lies behind this and I have only wished to give certain hints of these things. In studying St. Mark's Gospel we shall have to plumb depths of wisdom about which you will have to ponder for a very long time if hints are to lead to anything more. I will try to make clear to you in the following way how this Gospel should be read.

A rainbow appears to a child as something real in the sky and until it is explained to him, he thinks that he can touch and take hold of it with his hands. Later on he learns that a rainbow appears only when there is a certain combination of rain and sunshine; when the conditions of rain and sunshine change, the rainbow disappears. The rainbow is therefore not a reality in itself but only a mirage, an illusion; a combination of rain and sunshine is the reality.

Once we make a little progress on the path of occult knowledge we are likely to have an experience which will remind us of the sort of thing I have said about the rainbow, namely that ultimately there is in the external world no solid reality but only appearances which are sustained by factors outside themselves.—And do you know what this chimera is? It is man himself! Man himself is also such an appearance. If you take him as you see him with your physical senses as being reality, you are much mistaken. You are in fact surrendering to maya, to the great 'non-being'. The word 'maya' is derived from mahat aya—mahat = great; ya = being; a = non, negation; hence maya = the great non-being.

On the path of occult development a man reaches the point where he begins to think of himself as something like the rainbow. He is a chimera, like everything that comes before his physical senses. Even the Sun seen as a physical globe is a chimera. When physical science describes it as a globe of gas in cosmic space, that is good enough for practical purposes; but anyone who takes the globe of gas to be a reality is becoming a victim of maya, of illusion, of non-

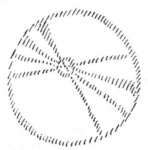

being. The truth is that the Sun is a meeting-place for Hierarchies of spiritual Beings, whose deeds come to expression in the warmth and light streaming from the Sun. The warmth and light themselves are an illusion; our other perceptions are also illusions. Normally we picture ourselves as having a heart in our breast; but that heart is nothing more than an appearance. What we see as a heart is rather like the rings we see around street lamps when we go out in the evening in an autumn mist; the rings are not really there but are the result of definite conditions. This is also true of the human heart. Imagine that this circle represents the vault of heaven and imagine various kinds of forces streaming in from different directions of the heavens and meeting at a particular point of intersection. In ultimate reality, where we think our heart is there is nothing but these heavenly forces that stream in and intersect. If you can somehow 'think away' everything except those instreaming forces, then the point of intersection actually is your heart. The same sort of thing is true of our other organs which are in reality only the outcome of intersecting cosmic forces.

Look at it from another point of view. When you move from one place to another you probably think that it is some impulse inside yourself that makes you move. If you do, then you are falling a victim to what we have called maya. The real fact is that there are forces streaming in from the Macrocosm which intersect, and thus evoke an illusion about the direction in which you are walking and the forces which make you walk. Down on Earth all that you really experience is the intersection of cosmic forces. If we want to get at the truth we have to find out what is going on in the Macrocosm and what the upper and lower cosmic forces are doing. Those forces create the effect of making us think we have a heart or a liver and talk as if we were going from place to place. If we want to express all this in terms of actual reality we should have to describe the movements of cosmic forces.

If we want to give an adequate description of the reality of the Baptism administered by John the Baptist, we should have to refer to what the cosmic forces—those symbolised in Aquarius—were requiring him to do. The ultimate decision had been taken in the great World Lodge and in consequence the necessary forces were sent into John. We must therefore read in the cosmic language accounts of what happened at a particular place on Earth. The writer of St. Mark's Gospel read in the heavens the processes corresponding to the events in Palestine. It is cosmic-astronomical events which he is describing, and so he says: Look at things in this way: here you have a wall on which you can see shadows playing, and if you want to know what 'causes' the shadows you must look upward to what is casting those shadows. I am giving you an account of what happened at the Jordan, but those happenings are really the means by which others are reflected on Earth. These things that I am describing come about through the interplay of macrocosmic forces active in the heavens.

The writer of this Gospel is therefore describing cosmic forces, phenomena and happenings in the heavens. And what he describes is the expression, the projection, the shadow-image cast by the happenings in the Macrocosm upon the little area of Palestine on the Earth. Only if we are quite clear about this will any real understanding of the greatness and significance of the Gospel of St. Mark be possible. We had first to form an idea of its contents and to understand what is said at the beginning, namely this: The prophet Isaiah foretold that the Lord of the soul-forces will come to men and that the 'messenger' will live in John the Baptist; he will prepare men for the approach of the Lord of the soul-forces.

This messenger had to take up his dwelling in the body of a man who had passed through the Aquarius Initiation. John could thus make possible on Earth the work of an individual such as Jesus of Nazareth; Jesus, on His side, had been prepared for the Pisces Initiation and through it was able to receive the Christ into himself.

Events on the Earth are the reflections of cosmic happenings, related to cosmic evolution as the rainbow is related to rain and sunshine. We must study rain and sunshine if we are to describe the true nature of the rainbow. And if we want to understand what lived in the heart of John the Baptist or in the heart of Jesus of Nazareth who became the vehicle of the Christ, we must study cosmic happenings. For the whole Universe was speaking to men in what took place in Palestine and on Golgotha. The Gospel of St. Mark as it stands merely provides the letters for accounts of mighty cosmic happenings. Whoever thinks otherwise is like someone who sees one set of ink-marks here and another there but has no conception of what the word 'Lord' signifies. The truth is that what is recounted in this Gospel amounts only to the letters—and moreover even they are an outermost shell. We must rouse ourselves to understand to what the events in Palestine are pointing, as it were in a play of shadows.

Try to grasp what is meant by saying that earthly events are shadows of macrocosmic events and you will then have taken the first step towards a gradual understanding of St. Mark's Gospel—one of the greatest sacred records in the world.

THE TWO MAIN STREAMS OF
POST-ATLANTEAN CIVILISATION

The last lecture began by speaking of the distinctive character of St. Mark's Gospel. It became clear that here, almost more than in the other Gospels, we can find in indications drawn from the deepest Christian mysteries, an opportunity to penetrate into many profound secrets and laws of the evolution of Man and of the Cosmos.

I had originally thought that during the winter it would be possible to make important and intimate references to matters of which we have not yet heard in our Movement, or perhaps better said, to matters at spiritual levels we have not yet reached. But we shall have to abandon this original plan for the simple reason that the Berlin Group has grown in numbers so astonishingly in recent weeks that it would now not be possible to make everything properly intelligible. We take it for granted that in mathematics and science some grounding is necessary if we want to reach a certain grade; and the same holds good to an even greater extent in the case of Spiritual Science. Later on, therefore, we shall have to consider how to present the parts of St. Mark's Gospel which are not suitable subjects for so large a Group.

In any attempt to understand a text such as that of the Gospel of St. Mark we must keep clearly in mind the factors which have influenced the evolution of humanity. I have always emphasised as a very general, abstract truth, that in all ages there have been certain leading figures among men who, because they were connected in some way with the Mysteries and with the spiritual, supersensible worlds, were in a position to implant into evolution certain impulses for its further progress. Now there are two main and fundamental

ways in which a man can establish relationship with
the supersensible worlds. One of these ways can be illus-
trated by the case of Zarathustra, the great Leader of mankind of whom I shall shortly be speaking in a lecture for the
public. The other way in which such Leaders of men
establish relationship with the spiritual worlds can be
envisaged if we think of the characteristic features of the path
followed by the great Buddha. These two outstanding figures
differ widely in the whole manner of their work and activity.

What Buddha and Buddhism call contemplation or meditation 'under the Bodhi tree'—a symbolic expression for a
certain mystical deepening of Buddha's consciousness—is a
path by which the human Ego can penetrate into its own,
inmost being. This path, opened up in so glorious a way by
the Buddha, is a descent of the 'I' into the depths, into the
abyss, of its own nature.

You will get a clearer idea of what this means if you
remember that we have followed the evolution of man
through four stages. Three of these stages have been con-
cluded and we are living now in the fourth. The first three
evolutionary periods were those of Old Saturn, Old Sun and
Old Moon, the fourth being that of the Earth proper. In the
first three periods man's physical, etheric and astral bodies
were brought into existence and in the present stage of
Earth-evolution his 'I', or Ego, is developing as an integral
member of his constitution. We have described the human
being from various points of view as an 'I' enveloped in three
sheaths—the astral sheath, the etheric sheath and the
physical sheath, deriving respectively from the three previous evolutionary periods of Old Moon, Old Sun and Old
Saturn.

At his normal stage of development to-day man has no
consciousness of his astral, etheric or physical bodies. You
will naturally insist that he is certainly conscious of his
physical body. But that is not so. For what is normally
regarded as man's physical body is an illusion, a maya.
What is taken to be the physical body is the product of the

interworking of the four members of man's constitution: physical, etheric and astral bodies, and the 'I'. As the product of this interworking the physical body is visible to the eyes and can be touched by the hands. If you want to see the physical body as it really is, you must isolate it, as in a chemical analysis, by separating off and disregarding the 'I' and the astral and etheric bodies. But present conditions of earthly existence make this impossible. Although you may think that it happens whenever a man dies, this is not correct. What a man leaves behind at death is not his physical body, but a corpse. The physical body could not exist under the laws which come into operation after death has taken place for these laws do not properly belong to it; they belong to the external world. If you follow these thoughts through to their conclusion you will have to agree that what is usually called man's physical body is the complex of laws by which the physical body is created within our mineral world, just as their own laws of crystallisation create, let us say, quartz or emerald.

The physical body of man functions as an organism in the mineral-physical world and this is the sense in which it is always spoken of in Spiritual Science. What we know of the world to-day is nothing but the result of what the senses perceive, and such perception is only possible in an organism in which there is an Ego, an 'I'. The superficial methods of observation now in vogue presume that an animal, for example, perceives the external world exactly as man perceives it through his senses. But this is a misguided view and people would be much astonished if—as will inevitably happen one day—they were shown how a horse, or a dog, or some other animal, pictures the world. If a picture were painted of the environment as perceived by a dog or a horse it would be very different from a man's picture of the world. We could not perceive the world as we do if the 'I' did not pour itself over the surrounding world, filling the sense-organs—the eyes, the ears, and so on. Only an organism in which an 'I' is present can perceive the world as man perceives it, and the outer human organism is itself an integral part of this picture. We must therefore conclude that what is usually called the physical body of man is only a result of our sense-observation, not the reality.

When we speak of physical man and of the physical world around him it is the 'I' that is viewing the world, with the help of the senses and the brain-bound mind. Hence man knows only that over which his 'I' extends, that which belongs to his 'I'. As soon as the 'I' cannot be present there is no longer any perception of the world-picture—in other words, man falls asleep. There is no picture of the world around him and he loses consciousness.

Wherever you look, your 'I' is bound up at every point with what you are perceiving; it is poured over the perception so that in reality you can know only the content of your 'I'. A normal man of modern times is aware of the content of his 'I' but he is not aware of his astral, etheric and physical bodies into which he penetrates every morning, for when he wakes he has no perception of his astral body. He would indeed be horrified if he had, for his astral body displays the sum-total of all the urges, desires and passions accumulated in the course of successive lives on Earth. Nor does he perceive his etheric body—there again he could not endure the sight. When he penetrates into his own intrinsic nature—into his physical, etheric and astral bodies—his attention is at once deflected to the external world; and there he sees what beneficent Divine Beings spread over the surface of his vision in order to safeguard him from descending into the core of his inner nature—an experience which he could not endure.

Therefore when we speak of this in terms of Spiritual Science, we rightly say that the moment a man wakes in the morning he passes through the portal of his own being. But at this portal stands a Watcher, the Lesser Guardian of the Threshold, who does not allow him to penetrate into his own being but diverts him immediately to the external world. Every morning a man meets this Lesser Guardian. Knowledge of him comes to anyone who, on waking, consciously passes into his astral, etheric and physical sheaths. And in the mystical life it is only a question of whether this Lesser Guardian benevolently dims our consciousness of our own inner being so that we cannot descend into it, diverting our 'I' to the environment, or whether he allows us to enter through the portal into our own nature and being. The mystical life consists essentially in passing the Lesser Guardian of the Threshold and entering into our inmost self.

In the case of the great Buddha, what is described symbolically as 'sitting under the Bodhi tree' is nothing else than this descent into the inner core of being through the portal that is otherwise closed. Buddhism describes what the Buddha had to experience in order to complete this descent. The narratives are not mere legends but presentations of deeply felt truths, profound realities experienced by the soul.

The experiences encountered by the Buddha in descending into his inmost nature are described as his 'temptations'. In his account of these temptations Buddha speaks of beings —even those he lo; ;—who draw near to him the moment he attempts the m stical descent; they urge him to some particular activity, for instance, to practise exercises which would lead him astray. We are told that the figure of the mother of Buddha appears to his spiritual vision and urges him to practise a false kind of asceticism. It was not, of course, his real mother; indeed his temptation consisted precisely in the fact that at the first stage of his developing vision, what appeared to him was an illusion, a mask. Buddha resisted this temptation and then a host of demonic figures appeared, who are described as the cravings one experiences in hunger and thirst or as passions, urges, pride, arrogance, vanity, ambition. All these forms confront him— but how? They still lurked in his astral body, in his astral sheath, but in his stronger moments, as he sat in meditation 'under the Bodhi tree', he had already overcome them. This temptation of the Buddha shows us in a wonderful way how all the forces and powers of our astral body produce their effect because through the downward trend of evolution in our successive incarnations, we have steadily deteriorated. In spite of the sublime height to which he had risen, the Buddha still saw the demons which tempt the astral body and at the final stage of attainment he had perforce to conquer them.

When a man descends through the region of the astral body, through temptations, into the physical and etheric bodies—when, that is to say, he really gets to know these two members of human nature, what does he find? Our attention must here be called to experiences connected with the descent. In the course of his incarnations on the Earth, man has been able to do severe damage to his astral body, but less damage has been caused to his etheric and physical bodies. The astral body is injured by all lower urges, by every form of egoism in human nature—envy, hatred, selfishness, arrogance, pride, and so on. A normal man of to-day cannot do much more in the way of injury to the etheric body than through lying or at most through unconscious error. But even so, only a part of the etheric body can sustain injury. A certain part of the etheric body is so strong that however hard a man might try to injure it, he would be unable to do so; it would always resist. Through his individual powers a man cannot descend deeply enough into his own nature to be able to injure the etheric or the physical body. It is only in the course of repeated incarnations that the faults for which he is directly responsible have an effect upon these bodies and then they appear as illnesses, defects and dispositions to illness in the physical body. But a man cannot work directly from his individuality upon his physical body. A cut finger or a bodily infection is not the result of any activity of the soul. In the course of his incarnations man has become capable of working upon the astral body and part of the etheric body; but upon his physical body he can work indirectly only, never directly.

Hence we can say that when a man descends into the region of the etheric body upon which he still has some direct influence, everything that is part of him from his successive incarnations becomes manifest. By sinking into the depths of his own being, a man finds the way to his incarnations in the near or more distant past. And when the descent is as intense and complete as it was in the case of the great Buddha, this vision of the incarnations extends farther and farther.

Man was originally a wholly spiritual being. In course of time sheaths gathered around this spiritual being. Man was born out of the spirit, of which everything external is a condensation. Hence through penetrating into his own being he finds the way to the spirit of the universe. This descent into the sheaths enfolding the physical body is a path leading to the spiritual texture of the universe, enabling man to see how the physical has been built up in the course of his incarnations. And when he can go far enough back into the past, to the times when with his primitive clairvoyance he was in a certain respect one with the spiritual world, he then had direct vision of that world.

In tradition—which again is not merely legendary—we learn of the stages reached by the Buddha as he penetrated through his own being. Of these stages he himself says: When I had attained the stage of Illumination—that is to say, when he could feel part of the spiritual world—I beheld that world outspread before me like a cloud; but as yet I could distinguish nothing in it, for I was not yet perfect. I advanced a step further and then not only could I see the spiritual world outspread like a cloud but I could distinguish particular forms. But still I could not see what the forms actually were, for I was not yet perfect. Again I ascended a step and now not only could I distinguish the spiritual Beings but I could also recognise what order of Beings they were.—This process continued until the Buddha beheld his own archetype which had passed down from incarnation to incarnation, and could see its true relationship with the spiritual world.

This is the one way, the mystical way; it is the descent

through a man's own nature and being to the point where the bounds beyond which lies the spiritual world are broken through. It is by following this path that certain leading Individualities acquire the powers they need in order to give an impetus to the evolution of humanity.

Very different is the path by which men such as the original Zarathustra came to be leaders of mankind. If you will recall what I have said about the Buddha, you will realise that having become a Bodhisattva in his earlier incarnations he must already have risen through many stages. Through the illumination known as 'sitting under the Bodhi tree'—an expression which must be understood in the sense I have indicated—a man can develop vision of the spiritual worlds and rise to great heights through the faculties of his own Individuality. But if humanity had always been obliged to depend upon leaders of this kind only, the progress that has actually been made would not have been possible. There were leaders of a different type altogether, of whom Zarathustra was one. I am not speaking now of the *Individuality* of Zarathustra but of the 'personality' of the original Zarathustra, the herald of Ahura Mazdao. If we study such a personality at the point where he stands in world-history, we realise that this is not a human being who has risen through his own intrinsic merits. On the contrary, he is a personality who has been chosen to be the bearer, the sheath, of a spiritual Being who cannot himself incarnate in the flesh, who can only send his illumination into and work within a human sheath.

In my Rosicrucian Mystery Play, *The Portal of Initiation*, I have indicated how at a certain point of time, when it is necessary for world-evolution, a human being is inspired by a higher spiritual Being. This is not poetic imagery but a poetical presentation of an occult reality.

The personality of the original Zarathustra was not one which through its own merits had reached as lofty a stage of development as that attained by Buddha; the personality of Zarathustra was chosen to be the abode of a higher Being and was filled with living spirituality. Such personalities were chiefly to be found in the early, pre-Christian civilisations which had arisen throughout Europe, in North-Western and Mid-Western Asia but not in the other civilisations which spread through Africa, Arabia and Asia Minor, into Asia. In these latter territories the predominant mode of Initiation was the one I have just described as having been achieved in its highest form by the great Buddha. Taking Zarathustra as a particular example among the peoples of the Northern stream, I shall now speak of the mode of Initiation which was to be found, too, in our own part of the world. Three or four thousand years ago this was the only kind of Initiation that it was possible to attain.

The personality of Zarathustra was chosen in somewhat the following way to be the bearer of a higher Being who was not himself actually to incarnate. It was decreed by the higher worlds that into this child there was to descend a divine-spiritual Being who when the child matured could work in him, make use of his brain, his faculties and his will. —To this end the circumstances of the life of such a human being must be quite different from those otherwise prevailing in the development of an ordinary individual. The happening I shall now briefly describe must be thought of as belonging to the whole life of such a human being, not confined to the physical realm of sense. Although the symptoms will not be perceptible to the ordinary senses, it will be clear to anyone with finer powers of observation that from the very beginning there is evidence of conflict between the soul-forces of such a child and the external world; that in this child there is a will and an inner driving power at variance with what goes on in the environment. But such is the destiny of a personality thus filled with a divine-spiritual Being. He grows up as a stranger, for those around him have no insight or feelings which would help them to understand him. Generally there are only very few—perhaps only one—with any inkling of what is developing in such a child. On the other hand, conflicts with the world around will easily arise and in such a case what I described to you in the story of the temptations accompanying Buddha's descent into his own being, will take place at an earlier age of life.

In the normal way the individuality of a human being is born into the sheaths provided by his parents and his people. These sheaths do not always entirely conform with the individuality and on this account such men feel a certain dissatisfaction with destiny. A conflict of such force and intensity as was associated, for example, with Zarathustra, could not be endured by an individuality developing in the normal way. When a child such as Zarathustra is observed clairvoyantly he will be found to have feelings, faculties and forces of thought which will be quite different from those developing in the people around him. Above all it will be evident—it is in fact always evident but it passes unheeded because little attention is paid nowadays to the life of soul-and-spirit—that those around such a child know nothing about his real nature; on the contrary, they feel an instinctive hatred of him; they can make nothing of what is developing within him. There is no sharper conflict visible to clairvoyance than that between a child born to be a saviour of mankind and the storms of hatred that are unleashed around him. This is inevitable, for it is just because such a child is different that the great impulses can be given to humanity. Similar stories are also told about personalities other than Zarathustra.

The story goes that as soon as he was born, Zarathustra could smile—something that is usually not possible for several weeks. We are told that Zarathustra's smile came from his consciousness of the harmony of the world. The smile was said to be the first sign of the difference between this child and all the others around him.

There is a second story, to the effect that an enemy, as it were another Herod, named Duransarun, lived in the region where Zarathustra was born and that when the birth of the child was divulged to him by Chaldean Magi, he tried to kill the infant with his own hands. The legend tells that as he

raised the sword his arm was paralysed and he was obliged
to give up the attempt.—These are pictures of spiritual
realities which could have been revealed only to supersensible consciousness. We are further told how this enemy of the
infant Zarathustra then caused him to be carried by a
servant out into the desert to become the prey of wild
beasts. But when a search was made it was found that no
wild beast had touched the child and that he was sleeping
peacefully. This attempt having also failed, the child's
enemy caused him to be laid where a herd of cows and oxen
would pass and trample him to death. Instead, so the legend
tells, the first beast took the child between its legs, carried
him off and set him down when the whole herd had passed
by. The same thing was repeated with a herd of horses. And
the enemy's final attempt was to expose the child to wild
animals robbed of their young. But when the parents sought
news of the child they found that again the animals had done
him no harm: indeed according to the legend he had been
suckled by the 'heavenly cows'.

These indications are to be understood as showing that
through the presence of the spiritual Being, of the Individuality who passes into such a soul, very special forces are
called into play. Such a child is brought into disharmony
with his environment. This is necessary in order that evolution may be given an upward impetus. Disharmonies are
always inevitable if there is to be real progress towards per-
fection. It must also be realised that these forces help to bring
such a child into his destined relationship with the spiritual
world. But how does the child himself experience all these
conflicts?

Try to think of this penetration of a man's soul into his
own being, as an awakening. When the soul can experience
the physical body and etheric body it achieves the development we saw in the Buddha. But now imagine going to sleep
in full consciousness. As things are to-day, a man loses consciousness when he goes to sleep and the Void engulfs him.
But if he were to retain consciousness he would be surrounded

by a spiritual world into which his being pours. But here again there are obstacles. When we go to sleep, before the portal through which we must pass there also stands a Guardian. This is the Greater Guardian of the Threshold, who denies us entrance into the spiritual world as long as we are not ready for it. The reason for this is that if without being inwardly strong enough we attempt to pour our Ego over the spiritual world into which we pass on going to sleep, we face certain dangers.

The dangers are these.—Instead of perceiving objective reality in the spiritual world we should perceive only the effect of the fantasies which we ourselves take into that world; we take into it the worst that is in us—everything that is not in keeping with truth. Hence any premature entry into the spiritual world would mean that instead of reality, a man would see grotesque, fantastic images and forms, said by Spiritual Science to be a sight that does not belong to his humanity. Whereas if he had objective vision of the spiritual world he would reach a higher stage and would see what is human. It is always a sign that what are seen are fantasies if on rising into the spiritual world, animal forms appear. These animal forms are indications of our own irresponsible play of fancy; they appear because inwardly we have not a firm enough foundation. Faculties in us which at night are unconscious must be strengthened if we are to have a really objective vision of the outer spiritual world. Otherwise we see it subjectively and we take our fantasies into it. They do, of course, accompany us, but the Guardian of the Threshold protects us from sight of them. To be surrounded by animal forms which attack us and try to force us into error as we ascend into the spiritual world is all a purely inner process. To enter the spiritual world safely we need only develop greater and greater strength.

When an infant such as the Zarathustra-child is filled by a higher Being the little body is naturally immature and has to develop to maturity. The organic system of intellect and sensory activity is also disturbed. Such a child is in a world in which he may truly be said to be 'among wild beasts'. I have often emphasised that in descriptions of this kind the historical and pictorial elements represent two aspects of the same thing. The happenings take place in such a way that when the spiritual forces work from outside in the form of hostility, as in the case of the Zarathustra-child, they are personified in the figure of King Duransarun. Everything also exists in archetype in the spiritual world and the external events correspond to what is taking place in that world. It is not easy for the modern mind to grasp such a thought. If we say that the events occurring around Zarathustra have significance in the spiritual world, people think that they cannot be real. If we show that the events are authentic history, we then incline to regard the personality concerned as being no more highly developed than anyone else. Thus the liberal theologians of to-day tend, for instance, to regard the figure of Jesus of Nazareth as on a par with, or not greatly excelling, what they may picture as their own ideal. It disturbs the lazy materialism of men's souls if they have to picture a really great Individuality. There must not be anything in the world superior to the professor or theologian seeking to attain his own ideal! In dealing with great events, however, we are concerned with something that is both historical and symbolic; the one aspect does not exclude the other. Those who do not understand that external events have a significance other than their surface appearance will never grasp their essential reality.

The soul of the infant Zarathustra was actually exposed to great dangers; but at the same time, as the legend relates, the 'heavenly cows' stood at his side to succour him and give him strength.

Similar stories can be found over the whole area from the Caspian Sea, through our own region, and into Western Europe, in connection with all great founders of world-conceptions. Such personalities, without having risen to lofty heights through their own development, are indwelt by a spiritual Being in order to become leaders of men. There were a number of such traditions among the Celts. It is related of Habich, an important figure in Celtic religion, that he too was exposed to dangers and suckled by heavenly cows; that he was attacked by hostile animals who had to give way before him. The descriptions of the perils confronting Habich, the Celtic leader, read just as if extracts had been made from the seven 'miracles' of Zarathustra—for Zarathustra is to be regarded as the greatest personality among leaders of this kind. Certain features of his miracles are to be found all through Greece and on into the Celtic regions of the West. As a well-known example you have only to think of the story of Romulus and Remus.

This is the second way in which leaders of mankind arise. Certain deeper features of the two great streams of culture in the post-Atlantean epoch have now been characterised. After the great Atlantean catastrophe, one of these streams of civilisation spread and developed through Africa, Arabia and Southern Asia; the other spread in a more Northerly course through Europe, to Northern and thence to Central Asia. There the two streams united; and the outcome is our post-Atlantean culture. The Northern stream had leaders such as I have described in the figure of Zarathustra; in the Southern stream, on the other hand, there were leaders of the type revealed in its loftiest form by the great Buddha.

If you now recall what you already know about the Christ-event, you will want to understand what really happened at the Baptism by John in the Jordan. As in the case of all the leading figures and founders of religious thought in the Northern stream—of whom Zarathustra had been the greatest—a divine-spiritual Being, the Christ, descended into a human being. The process was the same but carried out at the highest level. Christ descended into a human being in his thirtieth year, not in his childhood, and the personality of Jesus of Nazareth was specially prepared for this event. In the Gospels the secrets of both types of leadership are shown us in synthesis, in harmony with each other. Whereas the accounts of the Evangelists St. Matthew and St. Luke are mainly concerned to show how the human personality into whom the Christ entered had been evolved, the Gospel of St. Mark describes the nature of the Christ Himself, the element in this sublime Individuality which could not be confined within the human vehicle. That is why the Gospels of St. Matthew and St. Luke describe with wonderful clarity a story of temptation different from that related by St. Mark. He is describing the Christ who had entered into Jesus of Nazareth. The Gospel of St. Mark relates the story of temptation which occurs in other cases already in childhood —the encounter with wild animals and the help given by spiritual powers. Thus it can be regarded as a kind of repetition of the Zarathustra-miracle when St. Mark's Gospel narrates in simple and impressive words: 'And immediately the spirit driveth him into the solitude (wilderness) . . . and he was with the wild beasts; and the Angels'— that is, spiritual Beings—'ministered unto him.' St. Matthew's Gospel describes a quite different process, one which seems like a repetition of the temptations of Buddha, that is to say the tests and allurements confronting the soul of a man who is penetrating into his own inner being.

The Gospels of St. Matthew and St. Luke describe the path taken by the Christ when descending into the sheaths He received from Jesus of Nazareth. St. Mark's Gospel describes the kind of temptation which the Christ was obliged to undergo when He confronted the environment—as happens with all great founders of religion who had been inspired from above by a spiritual Being. Christ Jesus experienced both these kinds of temptation, whereas earlier leaders of humanity had experienced only one. Christ united in Himself the two ways of entering the spiritual world.— That is the all-important point. What had formerly taken place in two separate streams into which smaller streams then flowed, was now united in one.

It is only from this point of view that we can understand the apparent or real contradictions in the Gospels. The writer of St. Mark's Gospel had been initiated into Mysteries which enabled him to describe the temptation presented in his Gospel, namely the encounter with wild beasts and the help of spiritual Beings. St. Luke was initiated into the other aspect. Each of the Evangelists writes of what he knew and understood. Hence their Gospels present different aspects of the events in Palestine and of the Mystery of Golgotha.

In all this I have been wanting to indicate from a point of view we have not hitherto adopted, how we have to understand the course of the evolution of humanity and the intervention of particular Individualities: whether those who rise from the rank of Bodhisattva to that of Buddha, or those whose significance lies not so much in themselves as in what has come down into them from above. It is in the figure of Christ alone that these two types unite; and it is only when we know this that we can rightly understand the Christ.

It will now be clear why incongruities are apparent in mythical personalities. When we are told that one of them behaved in a matter of right or wrong as, for instance, Siegfried behaved, someone will certainly protest that after all, he was said to have been an Initiate! But in the case of a personality such as Siegfried, through whom a spiritual Being was working, the individual development is not a factor that comes into consideration. Siegfried may well have had faults. What really mattered was that an impetus should be given to the evolution of humanity, and for this purpose it was a question of choosing the most suitable personality. The same standard cannot be adopted universally and Siegfried cannot be judged as you would judge a leader arising from the Southern stream of culture, for a figure such as Siegfried differs radically in character and type from men who penetrate into their own inner self.

It can therefore be said that the leading figures belonging to the Northern stream are permeated by a spiritual Being who drives them out of themselves, enabling them to rise into the Macrocosm. Whereas in the Southern cultures a man sinks into the Microcosm, in the Northern stream his being pours into the Macrocosm and in this way he comes to know all the spiritual Hierarchies, as Zarathustra came to know the spiritual essence of the Sun.

We may therefore sum up all that has been said, as follows.—The mystical path, the path of the Buddha, leads to such depths in a man's inmost being that in breaking through to them he comes into the spiritual world. The path of Zarathustra draws a man out of the Microcosm and his being is diffused over the Macrocosm so that its secrets become transparent to him. The world has as yet little understanding of the great spirits whose missions are to unveil the secrets of the Macrocosm. There is very little understanding, for example, of the essential nature and being of Zarathustra. And we shall find how greatly what we have to say of him differs from what is usually said at the present time.

This again is a digression intended to convey to you the intrinsic character of St. Mark's Gospel.

THE SON OF GOD AND THE SON OF MAN.
THE SACRIFICE OF ORPHEUS

The verses in St. Mark's Gospel which we were en-
deavouring to elucidate in the last lecture are followed by
remarkable words in many ways similar to those found in the
other Gospels, although their full significance can best be
studied in that of St. Mark. The words are to the effect that
after the Baptism and the experiences in the 'wilderness',
Christ Jesus went into the synagogue and taught the people
there.

The sentence is usually translated: 'And they were
astonished at his doctrine: for he taught as one that had
authority, and not as the scribes.'—To a man of the present
age, however orthodox a believer in the Bible, this sentence
conveys little more than that His teaching was powerful and
impressive—unlike that of the scribes. But in the Greek text
the sentence translated 'as one that had authority and not as
the scribes', is: ἦν γαρ διδάσκων αὐτοὺς ὡς ἐξουσίαν ἔχων, καὶ οὐχ
ὡς οἱ γραμματεῖς
(ēn gar didaskōn autous hōs exusiān echōn, kai ouch hōs hoi grammateis)
If we try to grasp the meaning of this significant passage
we shall be led a step further towards understanding the
secrets of Christ's mission. I have already called your
attention to the fact that like other genuinely inspired
writings, the Gospels are not easy to understand and that to
grasp their real meaning we must bring together all the
thoughts and ideas about the spiritual world acquired in
the course of many years. Such ideas alone can give us
insight into what is meant when it is said in the Gospel that
He taught in the synagogue as one of the *Exousiai*, as a

Power and Revelation, and not as those who are here called: γραμματεῖς (scribes).

To understand a passage such as this we must remind ourselves of what we have learnt about the higher, super-sensible worlds. We have learnt that man, as he lives in our world, is the lowest member of a hierarchical Order, that his place is at the lowest step of the ladder of this Order. Immediately above him in the supersensible world, at the first level, are the Beings called in Christian esotericism, *Angeloi*, Angels. They are the supersensible Beings of the rank immediately above man, who influence his life. Above them come the *Archangeloi* or Archangels, then the *Archai* or Spirits of Personality; then the *Exousiai, Dynameis* and *Kyriotetes*, and finally the *Thrones, Cherubim* and *Seraphim*.

Thus above man there are nine ranks of hierarchical Beings. And we shall now try to picture how these different supersensible Beings intervene in human life.

The Angeloi are the Beings who as messengers of the spiritual world to the individual man in his life on Earth, are nearest of all to him. They exercise a perpetual influence upon the destinies of individuals on the physical plane. The Archangeloi are spiritual Beings whose activities embrace a wider sphere. They are the Beings whom we may call 'Folk-Spirits', who regulate and guide the affairs of whole groups of peoples. When a man of the present day speaks of a 'Folk-Spirit' he thinks, purely in terms of number, of so many thousands of individuals who happen to populate the same territory. But in Spiritual Science we mean by a Folk-Spirit the actual Folk-Individuality, not such and such a number of people but a real individuality just as we speak of an individuality in the case of a single man. The spiritual guidance of a whole Folk lies in the hands of the Archangelos. All these higher Beings are supersensible entities having their own spheres of activity. The Archai, Spirits of Personality or the 'Primal Beginnings', are again different from the Archangeloi or Folk-Spirits. If we speak of the French, the German, the English Folk-Spirit and so on, this points to different regions of the Earth. But there is something that is common to all men to-day, at least to all Western peoples, and affords them a basis for mutual understanding. In contrast to the single Folk-Spirit we speak here of the Time-Spirit: there is a Time-Spirit in the period of the Reformation, another in our own day. The Time-Spirits, the Archai, rank above the individual Folk-Spirits, and are the leaders of successive epochs.

At a still higher level we come to the Exousiai. They are supersensible Beings of an essentially different order. To form an idea of how the Beings of these still higher Hierarchies differ from the Angeloi, Archangeloi and Archai, let us remind ourselves that there is no essential difference between a member of one Folk and a member of a different Folk as regards his outer, physical make-up and what he eats and drinks. It cannot be said that, except as regards soul and spirit, the peoples differ essentially from each other. The guiding spiritual Beings (the Time-Spirits) of the successive epochs are concerned with things of the soul and spirit only. Man does not, however, consist only of soul and spirit. It is the human astral body that is essentially influenced by whatever is of the nature of soul and spirit. There are also denser members of man's being which do not differ greatly from each other as far as the activities of the Angeloi, Archangeloi and Archai are concerned. But creative influences are exercised upon these denser members of man's nature by spiritual Beings belonging to ranks from that of the Exousiai upwards. Language and current modes of thought belong to the sphere of the Folk-Spirits and the Time-Spirits— Archangeloi and Archai. But men are also influenced by the light and air and climate of a particular region. One type of human being thrives below the Equator, another in the regions nearer to the North Pole. We shall not agree with a German professor of philosophy whose view, presented in a very widely read book, was that civilisations of essential importance would have to develop in the Temperate Zone because the human beings responsible for such culture

would freeze at the North Pole and scorch at the South Pole!
But we can certainly speak of the different effects of food
upon human beings living in different climates. External
conditions are by no means without influence upon the
character of a people—for example, whether they live in
mountain valleys or on plains. We see there how the forces of
nature penetrate into and affect the whole of man's constitution. Knowing from Spiritual Science that supersensible
Beings are active in all the forces of nature and work upon
men through these forces, we can make a distinction between
Archai and Exousiai, and say: The Angeloi, Archangeloi
and Archai influence man through what concerns the soul and
spirit only—language, current modes of thought, ideas, and
so on, but they do not work through the forces of nature;
their operations do not directly affect the etheric body or the
physical body, which are the lower members of man's
organism.

On the other hand, spiritual Beings from the rank of the
Exousiai upwards work not only upon man but also in the
forces of outer nature; they are the 'Directors' as it were of
air and light, of the different ways in which foodstuffs are
produced in the kingdoms of nature. They are the Beings
who hold sway in these kingdoms of nature. The phenomena
of thunder and lightning, rain and sunshine, how one kind
of foodstuff grows in one region, other kinds in another, in
short the whole ordering of earthly conditions we ascribe to
spiritual Beings of the Hierarchies higher than the Angeloi,
Archangeloi and Archai. We see the effects of the activity of
the Exousiai, for example, in the light that works upon us as
well as upon the plants, not only in the invisible effects which
are the manifestations of the Time-Spirits.

Let us now consider what it is that civilisation gives to men,
what they have to learn in order to make progress. Every
individual has at his disposal what is yielded by his own
epoch, but also, to a certain extent, the fruits of earlier
epochs. Now it is only what derives from the lowest Hierarchies up to and including the Time-Spirits that can be

preserved as history and be taught and studied as such. What streams directly from the kingdoms of nature cannot be preserved in tradition. Nevertheless, men whose powers of knowledge enable them to penetrate into the supersensible worlds can pass beyond the Time-Spirits to still higher forms of revelation. Such revelations are recognised as belonging to a realm higher than that of the Time-Spirits, as having greater weight than anything deriving from the Time-Spirits, and as affecting men in a very special way. Every rational human being should ask himself now and then whether his soul is affected more profoundly by what can be learnt from the traditions of the several peoples and Time-Spirits of historical epochs, or by a glorious sunrise, which is a direct manifestation of nature and of the supersensible worlds. Individuals may well become conscious that a sunrise in all its glory can stir the soul infinitely more deeply than all the science, the learning and the art of the ages. Suppose we have been deeply moved by the works in the Italian Galleries of Michelangelo, Leonardo da Vinci, Raphael and others, and later on climb some Swiss mountain and contemplate the spectacle there presented, we shall be vividly conscious of what nature can reveal. We shall ask: Who is the greater artist: Raphael, Leonardo da Vinci, or the Powers who have painted the sunrise to be seen from the Rigi?—And the answer can only be that wonderful as are the achievements of men, what comes before us as a revelation of divine-spiritual Powers is far greater.

Now when the spiritual leaders of mankind, the Initiates, appear before the world, their teachings are not based upon or drawn from tradition but flow from original sources anf. their revelations are like the revelations of nature herseld What is merely repeated by others can never have an effect as powerful as that of a sunrise. Compared with what tradition has handed down of the teachings of Moses or Zarathustra and what the Time-Spirits and Folk-Spirits have communicated through forms of external culture, the effect made by nature herself is far the greater. It was only when the revelations of Moses and Zarathustra sprang from immediate experience of the supersensible worlds that their effect was as powerful as that of the revelations of nature. The wonderful thing about these original revelations to mankind is that they are like the revelations of nature herself. We should remember here that the Exousiai are the lowest Hierarchy of Beings who work in the forces and powers of nature.

What, then, was experienced by those who were gathered in the synagogue when Christ Jesus came among them? Hitherto they had been taught by the 'Scribes', by men who were cognisant of what the Time-Spirits and Folk-Spirits had communicated. To such teaching the people were accustomed. But now there came One who did not teach as the Scribes taught, whose words seemed like a revelation from the realm of the supersensible powers in nature, in thunder, or in lightning. Knowing that the higher the rank of the Hierarchies the greater are their powers, we can understand in all their depth these words in the Gospel of St. Mark.

If we can feel the supersensible reality behind the creations of men such as Raphael, Leonardo da Vinci and others of their calibre, we can still glimpse in the relatively small number of pictures that have come down to us, something of the original inspiration. Great works of art, works of spiritual genius, are always echoes of what was originally revealed. And if we can perceive something of what Raphael, for example, expressed in his pictures, or form a living idea of the work of Zarathustra, we shall be able to hear something of what comes from the Exousiai.

But in the teachings given in the synagogues by the Scribes, that is to say, by men whose knowledge stemmed from the Folk-Spirits and Time-Spirits, there was nothing that could even faintly echo direct revelations of nature. Hence these words in St. Mark's Gospel are an indication that in men living in those days an inkling was beginning to dawn that something entirely *new* was speaking to them; that through this man who came among them something revealed itself which was like a power of nature herself, like one of the supersensible Powers behind the phenomena of nature. Men began gradually to divine what it was that had entered into Jesus of Nazareth and was symbolised in the Baptism by John. The people in the synagogue were very near the truth when they said: When he speaks it is as though the Exousiai were speaking, not merely the Archai, the Time-Spirits, or the Folk-Spirits.

It is only through knowledge of Spiritual Science that we shall be able again to instil a full and living content and meaning into the barren abstractions abounding in modern translations of the New Testament, and to realise what is involved when efforts are made to penetrate to the core of the Gospels. Generations must pass before there can be any prospect of fathoming, even approximately, the deep meanings which our own times can dimly surmise. Actual investigation of a great deal in the Gospels will be possible only in the future.

Fundamentally, what the writer of St. Mark's Gospel wished to present was an elaboration of the teaching of Paul, one of the first to recognise the nature and essential being of the Christ through direct supersensible perception. We must understand what Paul actually taught and what he experienced through the revelation that came to him on the road to Damascus. Although the event is described in the Bible as a sudden revelation, those conversant with the real facts know that this kind of illumination can come at any moment to one who is striving to reach the spiritual world and that as a result of his experiences he becomes a changed man. And in the case of St. Paul it is abundantly evident that through the revelation at Damascus this was what happened.

Even a superficial study of the Gospels and of the Pauline Epistles will make it clear that St. Paul regards the Event of Golgotha as the central point of the whole evolution of humanity and that he links this Event directly with what is described in the Bible as the creation of Adam, the first man. St. Paul's teaching is to somewhat the following effect: The being we must call the spiritual man, the real man, of whom in the world of maya there is only an illusory image, came down in ancient Lemurian times to this world of illusion, facing the experiences he was to undergo in the flesh during successive incarnations. He became man in the form assumed throughout the Lemurian and Atlantean epochs and in post-Atlantean times until the coming of Christ. Then came the Event of Golgotha.

Paul was unshakably convinced after his vision near Damascus that in the Event of Golgotha something occurred that was exactly comparable with the descent of man into the flesh. For therewith the impulse was given gradually to overcome those forms of earthly existence into which man had entered through Adam. Hence Paul calls the Being who appeared in the Christ, the 'new Adam', whom every man can draw to himself through union with Christ.

Thus from Lemurian on into pre-Christian times we have to see the gradual descent of man into matter—whether we call him Adam or by some other name. Then he was given the power and the impulse to ascend again so that he might eventually return, enriched by the fruits of earthly existence, to the original, spiritual state that had been his before he descended into matter.

Now if we are to understand the essential meaning of evolution, we must not ask: Could man not have been spared this descent into matter? Why was it necessary for him to pass through different incarnations in order to re-ascend into the state that was his at the beginning? Such questions could spring only from complete misunderstanding of the spiritual meaning of evolution. For man takes with him from Earth-existence all the fruits of his experiences and is enriched with the content of his incarnations—a content that was not previously his.

Think, hypothetically, of a man descending and passing through his first incarnation: there he learns certain things. In his second incarnation he learns more; and so on through all the incarnations. Their course, to begin with, is one of descent: man becomes more and more deeply entangled in the physical world. Then he begins an ascent and can rise to the extent to which he receives the Christ Impulse into himself. One day he will find his way again into the spiritual world; but he will then take with him whatever he was able to acquire on the Earth.

And so Paul sees in the Christ the central point of the whole process of man's earthly evolution, the power that gives him the impulse to rise into the supersensible world enriched with all the experiences of life on the Earth.

But from this standpoint, how does Paul regard the sacrifice on Golgotha, the actual Crucifixion? It is not easy to relate to our modern ideas the way in which St. Paul—and also the writer of St. Mark's Gospel—understood the sacrifice on Golgotha, this most essential fact of human evolution. Before this can be attempted we must familiarise ourselves with the thought that man as he stands before us is a Microcosm, and we must study all the implications of this fact.

Two periods of development, each very different from the other, are apparent in man's life between birth and death in every incarnation. In various ways I have already called attention to the difference between the two periods—for our study of Spiritual Science is more systematic than people usually imagine. One of these periods lies between birth and the point at which an individual's memory begins. If you follow your memories back, you reach a certain point beyond which they cease. You were already in existence then and may have heard from your parents or relatives about your doings; hence you have some knowledge of them but you yourself remember nothing beyond a certain point of time. Normal remembrance breaks off at this point, the most favourable age for which is somewhere about the third year of life. Before that point of time a child is highly impression-able. Just think how much is taken in during the first, second and third years of life; yet modern man has no remem-brance at all of *how* the impressions were made.—Then

follows the period through which the thread of memory runs
continuously.

We must pay careful attention to these two periods of
development for they are very important in man's life as a
whole. We must observe the development of the human
being closely and accurately and avoid the prejudiced views
of modern science. The facts of science confirm what I have
to say, but we should not attach too much weight to biased
views that deviate widely from the truth. Close observation
of man's development makes it evident that his life as an
individual in society is conditioned by whatever forms part of
the thread of memory which begins, approximately, in the
third year. Within the span of this thread of memory lies
every principle by which we consciously direct our life; it
embraces whatever rules of conduct we consciously accept as
worthy to be followed. Our Ego has no consciousness of what
lies before this point; of that, nothing finds its way into the
thread of our conscious life.

Thus before our conscious life begins there are certain
years during which our relation with the surrounding world
is quite different from what it is later.

The difference is radical. Penetrating observation of a
child before the period back to which memory extends when
he is older, would show that in those first years he feels himself to be within the universal, macrocosmic, spiritual life. He
does not separate or isolate himself from that life but feels
part and parcel of the whole environment. He even speaks of
himself as others do. He does not say: 'I want', but, 'John
wants'. It is only later that he learns to speak of himself as
'I'. Modern child psychologists pick holes in this explanation
but the truth is not controverted by their arguments which are
just evidences of their lack of insight. In his earliest years a
child still feels part of the world around him; it is only at the
point from which his memories begin that he gradually
detaches himself from his environment as an independent
being.

It can therefore be said that the principles a man may

accept for the guidance of his life and the whole content of his consciousness belong to the second phase of development beginning at the point of time referred to. In the first phase he has a quite different relation to the environment; he feels much more closely connected with it. The only way to understand this thoroughly is to imagine what would happen if the form of consciousness which has produced this feeling of direct connection with the surrounding world in early childhood were to remain in later years. If that were the case human life would take a very different course. Man would not feel so isolated; even in later years he would feel himself to be an integral part, a member, of the Macrocosm, the Great World. As things are he loses his feeling of oneness with the Great World and believes himself to be isolated from it. In ordinary life this isolation comes into a man's consciousness in an abstract form only, for instance, in his egoisms, or in a tendency to shut himself off more and more within his own skin. The view that man's life is enclosed within his skin is complete nonsense. Whenever he exhales he becomes part of the outer world for the breath previously indrawn is now outside. Man's picture of himself is pure maya but his form of consciousness makes this inevitable. Human beings nowadays are neither particularly inclined nor indeed mature enough to understand karma. If, for instance, anyone gets his windows broken he is apt to take this as an offence directed against himself, and he is annoyed by it because he feels himself to be an isolated being. But were he to believe in karma he would feel related to the whole Macrocosm and would know that in point of fact it is we ourselves who have broken the windows. For in truth we are interwoven with the whole Cosmos and it is sheer nonsense to imagine that we are enclosed by our skin. But it is only in very early childhood that this feeling of oneness with the Cosmos exists; in later life it is lost at the point to which memory reaches.

It was not always so. In earlier times, by no means very long ago, the consciousness belonging to early childhood extended, in some degree at least, into the later years of a man's life. This was in the times of the ancient clairvoyance; and with it went a very different kind of thinking and a different way of expressing facts. This is an aspect of human evolution about which the student of Spiritual Science must be quite clear.

When a male child is born nowadays he is simply regarded as the son of his father and mother: and if he has no birth or baptismal certificate bearing the names of his parents to identify him as a citizen, nothing is officially known about him and in certain circumstances his very existence is questioned. To the modern mind a human being is simply the physical offspring of his father and his mother.

This was not how people thought in a past not so very far distant. Scholars and researchers to-day do not, however, know that in earlier times not only was men's thinking different but the content and implications of the words and designations used were different. Hence interpretations of ancient legends do not convey their real meaning. We are told, for instance, of Orpheus, a Greek singer. I refer to him because he belongs to the period several centuries before the rise of Christianity. We may think of him as the one responsible for the organisation of the Greek Mysteries. This fourth post-Atlantean epoch of which he was an important figure in the opening stage, was a preparation for the Christ Event and what humanity was to receive through it. Thus in Greece Orpheus was the great Preparer.

If a man of the modern age were to encounter a figure such as Orpheus, he would simply say: he is the son of such-and-such a father and such-and-such a mother—and science might possibly look for inherited characteristics. There is, for example, a bulky tome in which all the hereditary characteristics of Goethe's families are set forth in an endeavour to present him as the sum-total of those characteristics. That is by no means how people thought in the days of Orpheus. The man of flesh and his physical attributes were not what really mattered to them. The essential qualities were those that enabled Orpheus to be the leader

and organiser of pre-Christian Greek culture—certainly not
the physical brain or nervous system. The essential thing was
the fact that he had within him—in his own field of experience—a quality derived from the supersensible world and
united with the material-physical element provided by his
personality. The eyes of the Greeks were directed, not to the
physical figure of Orpheus descending from father and
mother, perhaps also from grandfather and grandmother;
this figure was more or less unessential, being merely the
outer expression, the sheath. The essential element was what
had descended from a supersensible source and had united
with a material entity on the physical plane. Hence a Greek
would have said to himself: When Orpheus is before me, the
fact that he descends from a father and a mother need hardly
be taken into account; what is of importance is that his
soul-qualities, which have made him what he is, stem from
the supersensible, from a supersensible reality which has
never hitherto had anything to do with the physical plane; a
physical-material element has here been able to unite with
the supersensible reality in his personality.—And because the
Greeks regarded a purely supersensible quality as the hall-
mark of Orpheus, they said he was the offspring of a Muse,
the son of Calliope, not of a physical mother but of a supersensible reality which had never had any previous connection with the physical and material.

But as the son of Calliope and nothing more than that,
Orpheus could have given expression only to manifestations
of the supersensible world. In keeping with the nature of the
age in which he lived, it was also his mission to give expression to what would be of service to physical life in that
epoch. Hence he was not only a mouthpiece for the Muse,
for Calliope, as in much earlier times the Rishis were merely
mouthpieces for supersensible Powers, but his own life gave
expression to the supersensible in such a way that the physical
world also was important to his life. His teaching was connected with and suited to the climate of Greece, to what was

part of outer nature in Greece—and so Orpheus was made the son of Oeagrus, the Thracian River-God.

This shows us that to the Greeks what mattered most in their view was what was living in Orpheus' soul. In those days men were characterised by the quality of their souls, by their spiritual value, not, as in later times, by saying: he is the son of so-and-so, or, he comes from such and such a town. It is very interesting to see how deeply involved the Greeks felt in the destiny of a man such as Orpheus, who descended on the one side from a Muse and on the other from a Thracian River-God. Unlike the ancient prophets, Orpheus was subject not only to supersensible influences but to material influences as well—to all the influences exercised by the physical-material world.

Now we know that man consists of several members: the physical body, the etheric body, the astral body and the Ego, the 'I'. A man such as Orpheus, descended from a Muse— you now know what that means—was still able to see into the spiritual world; but on the other hand, his capacity for experiencing the spiritual world was weakened by the life he led on the physical plane as the son of his father, the Thracian River-God.

The Leaders in the second and third post-Atlantean culture-epochs who became mouthpieces for utterances of the spiritual worlds were able to perceive their own etheric body separated from the physical. In the civilisations where ancient clairvoyance prevailed—and it was the same even among the Celts—when a man was to be made aware of something he was called upon to communicate to his fellow-men, it was revealed to him in this way: his etheric body emerged from the physical body and became the bearer of forces which streamed down into it. If those who proclaimed the utterances of the spiritual worlds were men, their etheric bodies were female and they consequently saw in female form whatever communicated messages to them from the spiritual worlds.

Now it was also the purpose of the legend to show that

although Orpheus was in direct contact with the spiritual Powers, as the son of a Thracian River-God there was always the possibility that he would be unable to retain what was revealed to him through his own etheric body. The more thoroughly he made himself at home in the physical world and lived his life as a son of his country, the more did his power of clairvoyance recede. The story relates that Eurydice, the transmitter of his revelations, his soul-bride, was torn away from him through the bite of an adder—a picture of his human failings—and carried off to the under-world. He could win her back only by passing through an Initiation.—Whenever we are told of a journey into the un-derworld, an Initiation is meant.—In order to win back his bride, Orpheus must pass through an Initiation. But he was already too closely enmeshed in the physical world. He had indeed acquired the capacity to make his way into the under-world, but on his return, when his eyes again encountered the sunlight, Eurydice vanished from his sight. Why was this? It was because on seeing the sunlight he did something that was forbidden him: he turned and looked back. That is to say, he disobeyed a strict command given him by the God of the underworld, namely, that physical man, living on the physical plane, must not look back beyond the point of time I have indicated, to the period of the macrocosmic experi-ences of childhood; if these experiences were to penetrate into the consciousness normal in later life, they would give rise to clairvoyance in its ancient form. Hence the command of the God of the underworld that no man may seek to pene-trate the mysteries of childhood, to remember where the Threshold is fixed.—But this was what Orpheus did, and he consequently lost the faculty of clairvoyance.

Something of great delicacy and subtlety in connection with Orpheus is set before us in this story of the loss of Eurydice. One consequence is that man is sacrificed to the physical world. With a nature still deeply rooted in the spiritual he is also, partially, the sort of being which it is his

destiny to become on the physical plane. And so all the
forces of the physical plane press in upon him and he loses
Eurydice, his own innocent soul—which it is the fate of
modern man also to lose. These forces tear Orpheus to
pieces; in a sense, he is sacrificed.

What is it, then, that Orpheus experienced as representa-
tive of the transition between the third and fourth epochs of
post-Atlantean culture? In the first place he experienced the
stage of consciousness which the child leaves behind—the
connection with the Macrocosm. This does not pass over into
his conscious life and therefore in his essential being man is
torn to pieces and killed by life on the physical plane which
in the real sense begins at the point of which we have been
speaking.

And now keep in mind this man living on the physical
plane; he is normally able to remember back only to a
certain point of time; beyond this lie the three years of
earliest childhood. With this thread of memory he is so
enmeshed in the physical plane that, in his own being, he
cannot endure it and he is torn to pieces. Thus it is with the
true spirit of man to-day—here is a proof of how deeply he
is enmeshed in matter. This is the spirit which in Pauline
Christianity is called the 'Son of Man'. Here is a concept
which you must grasp—the concept of the Son of Man who
can be found in a human being onwards from the point in his
life to which his later memory extends, and includes everything he has acquired from the civilisation around him.
Keep this 'man' in your mind, and then picture to yourselves
what he might become if there were added to him all that
presses in upon him from the Macrocosm in the first three
years of his childhood. This could be a foundation only,
because at that stage the developed human 'I' is not yet
present. But if it did merge into the consciousness of a
developed 'I', we should witness a happening comparable
with what took place at the Baptism in the Jordan at the
moment when the Spirit descended from above into Jesus of
Nazareth: the three innocent years of early childhood

merged with the rest of the human being. That is the immediate fact. And the consequence was that this innocent childhood-life, as it sought to develop on the physical Earth, could evolve for three years only—as is indeed always the case—and then met its end on Golgotha. It could not merge with what man becomes at the point in time from which in later life his memory normally begins.

Think what it would be like if, in one man, we saw mingled together all the interconnections with the Macrocosm which show themselves dimly and indistinctly in the early years of childhood but which cannot really light up in the child because he is as yet without Ego-consciousness. Think further, and picture to yourselves how, if the reality did dawn in this way in a later consciousness, something would take shape which has its origin, not in man's own nature but in the depth of those cosmic worlds out of which we are born. If you think of all this you will get an idea of the meaning of the words spoken in connection with the event portrayed as the descent of the Dove: 'This is my beloved Son; this day have I begotten him.' That means: Here the Christ is incarnated, begotten, in Jesus of Nazareth, born in him at the moment of the Baptism by John. In the Christ there was present, in its highest form, the consciousness otherwise belonging only to the early years of childhood; now, mingling with it, there was feeling of oneness with the Cosmos which a child would feel if it could be fully aware of its experiences during the first three years. In that case there would be still another meaning in the words: 'I and the Father'—that is, the cosmic Father—'are one'.

If you ponder deeply about these things you will get an inkling of what was experienced by St. Paul as a first, basic element in the revelation near Damascus and finds expression in the beautiful words: 'Except ye become as little children, ye shall not enter into the kingdom of Heaven.' Among many meanings of this saying there is the one indicated by St. Paul: Not I, but Christ in me—the Christ, that is, who has a macrocosmic consciousness such as a child would have if it could somehow combine the consciousness belonging to the first three years with the Ego-consciousness of later life. In the normal man of to-day these two forms of consciousness are separate: indeed they must be separate, for they are incompatible. Nor were they any more compatible in Christ Jesus Himself; after those three years, death was bound to supervene and to occur in the circumstances as they actually were in Palestine. These circumstances were not matters of chance but came about because these two lived within each other: the Son of God (which is man from the moment of his birth until the development of the Ego-consciousness) and the Son of Man (which is what he is after Ego-consciousness has been attained). The events which then culminated in the happenings in Palestine were the outcome of the living together of the Son of God and the Son of Man.

THE HIGHER MEMBERS OF MAN'S CONSTITUTION: THEIR RELATION TO THE PHYSICAL BODY AND TO THE OUTER WORLD

If, as I have proposed, we are to continue our study of certain matters relating to St. Mark's Gospel, we shall have to give a very wide interpretation to this aim; and it may be only after a considerable time that we shall see where a particular line of study belongs. To-day we shall speak of matters which, although they may seem to be remote from the main theme, will be of great help later on.

In the first place I want to emphasise that those who are not actually Members of our Movement, as long as they have not to some extent familiarised themselves with the real trend of spiritual-scientific thought, will always fail to understand what meaning and value any investigation based upon clairvoyance can have for people who as yet have no such faculties. It may well be asked: How can any belief in or conviction of spiritual truths come to those who cannot see into the spiritual worlds? Here we must keep on repeating that although it is not possible to see into the spiritual worlds as long as the eyes of clairvoyance are unopened, nevertheless the effects and manifestations of what is within those worlds are continually in evidence. For instance, when it is stated on the basis of clairvoyant investigation that man consists of four members—physical body, etheric body, astral body and Ego—someone to whom clairvoyant investigation means nothing, might say: I see only the physical body; how can I convince myself that what is said about the etheric and astral bodies is true before my karma makes it possible for me actually to see them? Now it is easy enough, if you so wish, to deny the existence of the astral body and etheric body; but the consequences of processes taking place in those bodies cannot be argued away because they are quite apparent in life. And in order that you may gradually come to understand that the structure of man's being and constitution is taken for granted in many expressions used in the Gospels, I want to-day to show you how the consequences of processes in the etheric or the astral body, for example, are clearly evident in everyday life on the physical plane.

Let us first of all consider the difference between a man who is full of idealism, who sets himself high ideals, and one who, generally speaking, lacks any such inclination, who acts only in response to external stimuli, eating when he is hungry, sleeping when he is drowsy and allowing instinct or desire or passion to drive him to whatever action he may take. Naturally there are any number of intermediate stages between the two types of men—those of the kind last described and those others whose purposes, thoughts and ideals infinitely transcend anything they are able to achieve in everyday life. Idealists such as this are in a peculiar position. They have to learn and to accept as a fact that in life on the physical plane our actions can never wholly conform with our highest ideals. An idealist always has to accept the fact that actions must inevitably fall short of his ideals. Strictly speaking, then, it must be admitted that in ideals there is always something loftier than actual deeds. From the standpoint of Spiritual Science the mark of the idealist is that his thoughts are loftier than his deeds.

Of the other type of individual the opposite can be said, namely, that his thoughts are of less account than his actions. A man who acts only out of instincts, passions, desires or similar urges, lacks the quality of thought that would be capable of comprehending the results of his deed at any particular moment; happenings to which he gives no thought at all ensue from what he does on the physical plane. His purposes and thoughts are narrower in scope and more restricted than his actions, his deeds, on the physical plane.

The clairvoyant has something to tell us about these two

types of men. When we perform a deed in life that is of greater importance than our thoughts, this deed always casts a reflected image, a mirror-picture, into our astral body: indeed after every single deed we perform an image, a picture, is left in the astral body. This image subsequently imprints itself on the etheric body and in that form remains perceptible in the Akasha Chronicle, so that a clairvoyant is able to see the reflected pictures of what a man has done during the course of his life. Similarly, when actions fall short of the fulfilment of the ideals, reflected pictures are left in the astral body and again impressed upon the etheric body. But there is one great difference between the reflected pictures of actions springing from instincts, desires and passions, and the reflected pictures of actions which are the outcome of idealism. The first contain something which endures as a destructive element in a man's whole life; they are images held in the astral body which react upon the whole human constitution and gradually undermine it; they are closely connected with the way in which a man in his life on the physical plane slowly undermines his forces until he dies. On the other hand, reflected pictures or images springing from thoughts that are loftier than our actions have life-giving properties. They are particularly stimulating for the etheric body and continually bring new life-giving forces into our whole constitution.

Thus according to the findings of clairvoyance we have within our constitution on the physical plane forces which destroy and also forces which continually impart new life. As a rule the effect of these forces in our lives can be easily observed. We meet human beings who are surly, hypochondriacal, morose in temperament, unable to come to terms with their own soul-life which in turn reacts upon their physical organism. They become apprehensive and uneasy, and anxiety, if it is persistent, manifestly undermines their physical health. In short, there are individuals who in their later years become melancholic, sullen, unable to adjust themselves inwardly and are in many respects unbalanced. If we were to look for the cause of bearing and conduct of this kind we should find that such individuals had little opportunity in earlier life to experience how idealistic thought can be loftier than action.

In everyday life these things are often unnoticed, although the effects cannot be denied. Many individuals feel the effects very strongly as the prevailing mood of their whole life of soul; they may even feel them in their bodily constitution. The existence of the astral body may be denied but not its consequences, for they are matters of actual experience. And when things of this kind can be observed in ordinary life, people ought to realise that it is not, after all, so very foolish to assert that although supersensible happenings and facts can be observed only by a clairvoyant, anyone can perceive their manifestations in actual life.

On the other hand, actions which inevitably fall short of their corresponding thoughts leave impressions which manifest themselves in later life as courage, confidence, balance. These qualities work right into the physical organism; but the connections will be perceived only if life is observed not in short sections but over a lengthy period. The error of many scientific observations is that conclusions about some effects are drawn on the basis of what happens in the course, say, of the next five years, whereas in many cases the effects show themselves only after decades.

But as well as individuals who are idealists, whose thoughts are loftier than a particular experience there are others whose thoughts always fail to keep pace with their experiences. There are very many experiences which can be grasped in thought only with the greatest difficulty. We eat and drink every day by instinct or as the result of desire: but it takes a very long time, even for one who is undergoing spiritual development, to relate these things too to the spiritual life. In point of fact, everyday things are more difficult than any others to bring into relation with the spiritual life. In the case of eating and drinking we shall have achieved this only when we have discovered why, in order to

serve the course of the world's evolution, we have to take
physical substances into ourselves in a rhythmic process, and
what connection these physical substances have with spiritual
life. We then find that metabolism is not a physical process
only, but by virtue of its rhythm also has in it something
essentially spiritual.

Now there is a way in which things not merely demanded
by external necessity can be gradually spiritualised. When
we are eating fruit, let us say, such spiritual knowledge as we
possess enables us to form an idea of how the fruit—an apple,
for instance—is related to the universe as a whole. Admittedly, however, this takes a long time. We can also train
ourselves to regard eating as being something more than a
merely physical activity and to remember how the spirit
participates by way of the sun's rays in the ripening of the
fruit. We can thus spiritualise the most material, everyday
processes and learn to penetrate them with our thoughts. I
can do no more than indicate here how thoughts and ideas
can penetrate into processes of this kind. It is a long business
and in our time very few people indeed can develop adequate
thoughts about eating.

We shall therefore admit that there are individuals who
act purely on the basis of instinct and others who act on the
basis of ideals. The life of every human being divides itself in
such a way that in some cases the thoughts cannot keep
abreast of the actions and in others the range of the thoughts
and ideals is greater than that of the actions. We have within
us, on the one hand, forces which lead our life into decline
and work in such a way that our physical organism matures
through inner causes towards death. And we have within us
other forces which bring life to our astral and etheric bodies
and shine out within them like a new light. It is these latter
forces which remain in our etheric body as life-giving forces.
When at death the spiritual part of our being abandons its
physical sheath, the etheric body is still around us during
the first few days, making it possible for us to have the backward
survey over our whole life of which I have often spoken.

The most valuable thing remaining to us as an inwardly formative, upbuilding power are these life-giving forces, originating from the fact that our ideas have transcended the bounds of our actions. These forces continue to work in us after death and actually provide further life-giving forces for the following incarnation.

Life-giving forces, then, implanted by ourselves, remain in the etheric body as an element that is always young. And although we cannot thereby prolong our life, we can enable the freshness of youth to remain for a longer period by ensuring that our thoughts transcend the range of many of our actions.

If we ask what is the best way of acquiring ideals which transcend our actions we shall find it possible if we devote ourselves to Spiritual Science. When, for instance, we learn from Spiritual Science of the evolution of man, forces are set astir in the higher members of our being and this gives rise to idealism in the most concrete, most balanced form. One of the achievements of Spiritual Science is to pour fresh, youthful, fertile forces into our astral and etheric bodies.

The very different attitudes to Spiritual Science adopted by individuals in this modern age are due not to the fact that these individuals have no clairvoyant faculties but that in everyday life their observation is not sufficiently exact. Otherwise they would see in what different ways the human soul and spirit manifest themselves in the physical organism. People who thoroughly disbelieve in Spiritual Science may hear that the physical body of man is somehow permeated by certain higher members. Let us take them together and simply call them the soul-and-spirit. But present-day materialists will not believe in the existence of this man of soul-and-spirit: they believe only in physical man and are in this respect particularly materialists. By 'materialists' people often mean simply the theoretical materialists, who believe only in matter. But as I have said again and again, these theoretical materialists are by no means the worst. A materialist may use his intellect just to create concepts;

they will in any case be very limited in scope and this form of materialism is not so very harmful. But when materialism is reinforced by other factors it can be very detrimental to the man's life as a whole—especially if the inmost, spiritual core of his being becomes dependent upon his material constitution. And nowadays, especially, how dependent men are upon matter! Theoretical materialism leads thoughts astray and is fatal to the ties that link souls together. But external life too is greatly influenced by the fact that so many people put materialism into actual practice. I mean by that, individuals who are so dependent upon their physical constitution that they can spend only a few winter months in their offices and in summer find it necessary to go off to the Riviera. The fact is they are so utterly dependent upon what is material that the soul has to subject itself to the needs which life dictates to it. That again is a different kind of materialist from a man who is materialistic only in his thoughts and ideas. Theoretical idealism may lead to the conviction that theoretical materialism is all wrong. But to cure practical materialists, to cure complete dependence upon the substances of the physical body, is possible only through genuine absorption in Spiritual Science.

If people could bring themselves to think—that is if their thoughts came not just from their intellect but were connected with reality—they would recognise from perfectly ordinary, everyday facts that there is a great difference between the various parts of man's being, for example between the hands and other parts of the body—the shoulders, let us say. A purely external investigation of man's physical body reveals differences in the action of the nerves. But it must be remembered that we can exercise a certain influence here. If the behaviour of the nerves were decisive for the soul we should be dependent upon material effects, for the action of the nerves is a material effect. But we are certainly not dependent in this respect, for influences of every kind can be brought to bear on the action of the nerves. The reason, quite simply, is that the etheric and astral bodies—the soul-and-spirit part of man—work in such very different ways. It is not enough to say that the physical body is filled with the etheric and astral bodies, for there is a difference that varies with the part of the body under consideration. We can easily convince ourselves that spiritual influences acting upon different parts of the body produce different effects. But we must be quite clear that what happens in life is under the sway of necessity. When there is something unusual about the direction taken by a current of air the physicist can apply his laws to discover the reason. But why is it that people do not reflect about the significance of the fact that they wash their hands far more often than any other part of the body? You will think it strange to introduce such matters; but it is these everyday phenomena that confirm the communications of a clairvoyant. It is also a fact that there are individuals who enjoy washing their hands as often as possible, and others who do not. Understanding of such an apparently trivial fact actually demands very advanced knowledge. To a clairvoyant the hands of a man are remarkably different in a particular respect from all his other bodily members. Luminous projections of the etheric body stream out from the fingers, sometimes glimmering faintly, sometimes flashing far into the surrounding space. The radiations from the fingers vary according to whether the man is happy or troubled and there is also a difference between the back of the hands and the palm. For anyone able to observe clairvoyantly, a hand, with its etheric and astral parts, is a most wonderful structure. But everything in our environment, material though it be, is a revelation, a manifestation, of the spirit. You should think of matter as being related to spirit as ice is to water; matter is formed out of spirit—call it 'condensed spirit' if you like. Contact with any material substance means contact with the spirit in that substance. All our contact with anything of a material nature is in fact—to the extent that it is purely material—maya. In reality it is *spirit* with which we come into contact.

If we observe life with sensitivity, we shall realise that

washing the hands—especially if it is done frequently—brings a man into contact with the spirit in the water and has a considerable effect upon his whole disposition. Some individuals have a great fondness for washing their hands; directly the least speck of dirt gets on their hands they must be washed! Such characters either have, or will develop, a very definite relation to their surroundings, a relation not entirely the outcome of material influences. It is as if delicate forces in matter were working upon such individuals when there is this relationship between their hands and the element of water. Even in everyday life you will find that these people have an entirely healthy kind of sensitivity and more delicate powers of observation than others. They are at once aware, for instance, whether someone standing near them has a brutal or a kindly disposition. On the other hand, individuals who do not mind their hands being dirty are actually of a coarser disposition and erect a sort of barrier between themselves and their environment. This is a fact and can actually be observed as being characteristic of certain groups. Travel through certain countries and observe their inhabitants. In regions where people tend to wash the hands more frequently, you will find that relations between friend and friend are very different from what they are in regions where people wash their hands less often and erect a sort of barrier between one another.

These things have the validity of natural law, though the details may be affected by various circumstances. If we throw a stone into the air the line of projection is a parabola; but if the stone is caught by a gust of wind there will no longer be a pure parabola. This shows that all the relevant facts must be known if certain relationships are to be accurately observed. As to the hands, clairvoyant consciousness reveals that they are permeated by soul and spirit—to such an extent, indeed, that a definite relationship of the hands to the water is established. This holds good less in the case of the human face and less still in the case of the other parts of the body. This must not, however, be interpreted as an objection to washing or bathing but rather that we must keep our attention fixed on the relevant circumstances.

The point here is to show how very differently the soul and spirit are related to and express themselves in the various parts of the body. You are not likely to find that anyone does harm to his astral body by washing his hands too often, but the point must be considered in its widest range. The relationship between hands and water may exercise a healthy influence on the relation between man and his surroundings, that is to say, between his astral body and his environment; and for this reason things will not readily be carried to extremes. But those who think materialistically and allow their thoughts to be attached solely to matter will say that what is good for the hands must be good for the rest of the body. This would show that differences depending on delicate perceptions entirely escape notice; the consequence —and it is abundantly in evidence—is that for certain purposes the same treatment is applied to the whole of the body. For instance, frequent cold baths and constant cold water frictions are recommended as a particularly effective treatment, even for children. Fortunately, because of obvious effects on the nervous system, doctors have already begun to realise that these treatments have been carried to absurd extremes. What is right for the hands because of their particular relation to the astral body can become an injurious experiment when applied to parts of the body having a different relation to the astral body. Washing the hands may bring about a healthy sensitivity to the environment; but an excessive use of cold baths and the like may cause an unhealthy hypersensitivity which, especially if such treatment is applied in childhood, lasts for the whole of life.

It is therefore all-important to know the limits within which methods may be beneficially applied; and this will be possible only if there is willingness to acknowledge that higher members of man's being are incorporated in his physical body. It will then be recognised that some of the inner organs used by the physical body as instruments are very differently related to the being of soul-and-spirit. It will be found, for instance, that the glandular system is preeminently the instrument of the etheric body, whereas everything associated with the nerves, for instance the brain, is intimately related to the astral body.

If these things are not kept in mind certain phenomena will always remain unintelligible. Materialists make the fundamental mistake of confining their observations to what in every case is only the instrument. For everything we experience is experienced in the realm of the soul; and our consciousness of these experiences is due to the fact that we have in the physical body an instrument which reflects them. Our physical body is only an instrument for reflecting what is going on in the life of soul. Anyone versed in Spiritual Science is clear about this. But the physical body can serve as an instrument in different ways. I need only point to one thing: the unique significance of the thyroid gland. As you know, the thyroid gland used to be considered a useless organ and in certain illnesses was often totally removed. In such cases the patients became imbeciles. The danger is substantially reduced if even a small part of the gland is left. This is evidence that the thyroid secretions are necessary for the development of certain aspects of the life of the soul. The strange thing is this: that if a secretion of a sheep's thyroid gland is administered to patients who have lost the gland, their condition is improved; if, later on, this treatment is discontinued, they lapse again into imbecility.

Materialists might find considerable support for their views in this fact. But the spiritual scientist knows how to judge it correctly. We are concerned here with an organ, the product of which can be introduced directly into our organism and be effective. But this can apply only to organs such as the thyroid gland, which are definitely related to the etheric body. Such an effect is not possible if the organ is related to the astral body. I have known poorly gifted individuals who have eaten plenty of sheep's brains but have not thereby become intelligent! This again shows that there is a great difference between the several organs, the magnitude of the difference being due to the fact that one group of organs has an inner connection with the etheric body and another with the astral body.

This reveals another important fact to spiritual observation. It seems very strange that a man may become feeble-minded if his thyroid gland is removed altogether but recovers his wits if he is given an extract of the gland. It is particularly strange because there is no evidence that his brain has been detrimentally affected. Here is another case where ordinary observation should be led on to spiritual-scientific observation. Spiritual Science shows that a man does not become an imbecile because his thyroid gland is removed. 'But', you will say, 'facts show that he does!' In reality, however, men do not become imbeciles because they cannot think, but because they are deprived of the possibility of using an instrument through which they become attentive to their environment. They are not imbeciles because they lack reasoning power but because they have no contact with their environment, and this insensibility is not the same as loss of reason. It does not necessarily follow that a man has lost his reason if he fails to exercise it because of lack of attentiveness to the environment. If you do not think about a thing you cannot express yourself about it; if you want to establish relationship with anything you must think about it. When the thyroid gland is removed a man's living interest in things is undermined—to such an extent indeed that he ceases to use his reasoning power.

Here you can see the subtle difference between using parts of the brain which are an instrument for the reasoning mind and using an instrument such as the thyroid gland. Light can thus be thrown on the ways in which the physical body is an instrument; and if we observe attentively we shall also be able to differentiate accurately between the several parts of man's constitution.

The 'I' is related to the surrounding world in the most varied ways. We shall be concerned here with certain facts which I have described elsewhere, showing that a man may endeavour to penetrate with his 'I' into his inner self, seeking to become aware of his own essential being; or he may turn to the external world, seeking to establish a connection with that world. We become conscious of the 'I' in a certain sense when we turn our attention inwards, when we reflect upon what life gives us or has in store for us. We can also become aware of the 'I' when, for example, we are brought into contact with the world outside by knocking against a stone, or perhaps when we cannot settle an account! We then become aware that our 'I' is unable to master the circumstances of external life. In short, we can become aware of our 'I' both in our inner life and when we are confronting circumstances of the external world. And we become aware of our 'I' in a very special way when the magical relationship we call sympathy or compassion is established with human beings or certain circumstances in our environment. There is clear evidence here of a magical process operating from soul to soul, from spirit to spirit. For we actually feel within ourselves something that is going on in the world outside, is being thought and felt there: we are experiencing in ourselves something that is of the nature of soul-and-spirit in the external world. We pass into the inner realm of our being in actual fact, for sympathy or compassion is an intimate experience in the life of soul. If our 'I' is not really equal to these experiences and needs to be inwardly strengthened, this comes to expression in the life of soul as sorrow, and physically as tears. Sorrow is an experience of the soul which gives the 'I' in the face of some external circumstance a feeling of greater strength than if it had remained indifferent. Sorrow always denotes an inner enhancement of the activity of the 'I'. Sorrow enhances the content, the intensity, of the 'I' and tears are an expression of the fact that the 'I' is at a particular moment striving to experience more than would have been possible had it remained indifferent.

We cannot but wonder at the poetic imagination that was already apparent in the young Goethe and was deeply connected with cosmic mysteries. I am referring here to the passage where Faust's weakness leads him to the point where he desires the physical extinction of his 'I', and he feels driven to suicide. Then the Easter bells ring out and at the sound of them the 'I' gathers strength; tears—the sign of sorrow in Faust's soul—burst forth and he cries: 'Tears start; earth holds me once more!' This indicates that what belongs to the earth has been strengthened; tears well up into the eyes, giving expression to the increased intensity of the 'I'.

Mirth and laughter too are connected with the strength or weakness of the 'I' in its relationship to the world outside. Mirth or laughter indicates that our 'I' feels more confident of its understanding and grasp of things and events. In laughter, our 'I' gathers such intensity that it pours itself out over the environment. This outpouring comes to expression in mirth, in the way we show amusement. Connected with this is the fact that—for the healthy-minded at all events—the cause of genuine sorrow must be a *reality*. Any reality in the external world which makes us feel as we participate in it that the inner activity of our 'I' must be enhanced, may induce a mood of sorrow. But if sorrow is associated with something unreal, for example, with some artificial representation given merely for the sake of arousing sadness, a man whose thinking is sound will require something more. He feels that what moves him to sorrow should arouse in him the surmise that what has caused the sorrow can be overcome.—I am merely hinting at this today and will deal with it more fully on another occasion.—A healthy soul feels the urge to rise to a higher level, to conduct itself worthily in the face of misery. Only a rather unhealthy soul will be satisfied with a mere representation of misery— unless in the representation there is implicit some prospect of victory. Thus we demand that in a drama there should be a prospect of victory for the victim of misery. No aesthetic can arbitrarily decree that only the trivial things in life shall be represented. But it will become evident that a man who follows his own healthy nature will not find that the demands of his 'I' are satisfied by an imitation of misery. The whole weight of reality is needed before the 'I' is roused to compassion.

And now think of this.—Is it not exactly the opposite as regards the comic? To laugh at real folly is in a certain respect inhuman. We cannot laugh at folly when it confronts us as reality. On the other hand it is thoroughly healthy to laugh at the representation of folly; and it was a very sound 'folk-therapy' to present to the people in comedy and burlesque how the folly of human action leads of itself to absurdity. When our 'I' is able in mirth or laughter to rise above what is recognised as folly in a given situation, it is strengthened by the spectacle of an artistic representation of folly, and there is no healthier laughter than this. On the other hand it is inhuman to laugh at a predicament in which a fellow human being finds himself, or at a real simpleton. Therefore different laws hold good if representation of these things is to have its proper effect.

If our 'I' is to be strengthened in an act of compassion, what moves us must confront us as reality. On the other hand, as healthy-minded men we demand, when misery is portrayed before us, that we should be able to feel the possibility of victory over it. In the dying hero of a tragedy, where death is enacted before our eyes, we feel that the victory of the spirit over the body is symbolised in this death. The very opposite is the case when the 'I' is brought into relation with the outside world. We feel then that we cannot fitly be moved to mirth or laughter when faced with reality, but rather that laughter is proper in cases that are removed from reality. We can certainly laugh when a man meets with a misfortune which does him no particular harm and is not closely related to life. But the more closely our experiences are related to reality, the less we laugh if we truly understand them.

From this it is clear that our 'I' is related to reality in different ways but the very variety of the facts testifies to the existence of a relationship even with what is most sublime.

You have heard in many lectures that in ancient Initiation there were two paths leading into the spiritual world: the one path was a descent into the inmost being of man, into the Microcosm; the other path led out into the Macrocosm. Now everything that comes to expression in great things is revealed also in the smallest. In ordinary life a man's descent into his inner being finds expression in sorrow, whereas the manner of his life in the external world shows itself in his ability to grasp the connection between processes that are apparently unconnected. Herein the supremacy of the 'I' is made manifest. And you have heard that if the 'I' is not to lose itself, it must be guided by an Initiation leading into the outer world; otherwise it will lose its bearings and may be led into what can only seem to be a void.

The smallest is connected with the greatest. Hence in Spiritual Science, where our thoughts are so often lifted to the highest spheres, we also concern ourselves with the most everyday matters. In the next lecture we shall turn once more to the consideration of higher things, making use of what we have been considering to-day.

LAWS OF RHYTHM IN THE DOMAIN OF SOUL-AND-SPIRIT. THE GOSPEL OF THE CONSCIOUSNESS-SOUL

When we study the Gospels in the light of Spiritual Science we find descriptions of momentous, overwhelming experiences. And it is only when Spiritual Science has been studied much more widely than it is to-day, that men will be able to form an adequate idea of what has been poured into these Gospels out of the spiritual experiences undergone by their authors. They will realise then that many things become apparent only when the accounts given in the four Gospels are studied side by side.

Let me first of all call attention to the fact that in St. Matthew's Gospel the account of the Christ Impulse is preceded by references to childhood and a record of the generations of the Hebrew people from their first ancestor onwards. In this Gospel the account of the Christ Impulse takes us to the beginning of the Hebrew people from whom the bearer of the Christ Being is born. In St. Mark's Gospel we meet the Christ Impulse at the very beginning. The whole childhood story is omitted. We are simply told that John the Baptist was the forerunner of the Christ Impulse and the Gospel then begins at once with the description of the Baptism by John in the Jordan. From St. Luke's Gospel we get a different childhood story which traces the ancestry of Jesus of Nazareth much further back, to the very beginning of humanity on Earth; the descent is traced to Adam who, it is then said, 'was the son of God'. This indicates clearly that the human nature in Jesus of Nazareth is to be traced right back to the time when man was formed from divine-spiritual Beings. Thus St. Luke's Gospel takes us back to an epoch when man must not be regarded as an earthly being incarnated in the flesh, but as a spiritual being born from the womb of divine spirituality. In St. John's Gospel, again without any childhood story or any mention of the destinies of Jesus of Nazareth, we are led in a very profound way to the Christ Being Himself.

In the course of the development of Spiritual Science we have followed a definite path in our study of the Gospels. We began with the Gospel which reveals the very highest insight into the spirituality of Christ—namely, the Gospel of St. John. Then we studied the Gospel of St. Luke, in order to understand how the highest spirituality in human nature reveals itself when man's descent is traced back to the time when he came forth, as earthly man, from the Godhead. Study of St. Matthew's Gospel then helped us to understand the Christ Impulse as proceeding from the ancient Hebrew people. Study of St. Mark's Gospel has been left to the last. To understand the reason for this, many subjects recently touched upon must be connected both with facts already familiar to us and with others that are new. That is why in the last lecture I said something about aspects of human life in connection with the several members of man's being. I shall be speaking in a similar strain to-day, as a kind of introduction to certain aspects of evolution. For it will become more and more necessary to recognise the conditions upon which human evolution depends—indeed not only to recognise but also to heed them.

As they advance into the future men will become more and more independent, more and more individualistic. Belief in external authorities will be increasingly replaced by belief in the authority of a man's own soul. This is a necessary trend of evolution. If, however, it is to bring wellbeing and blessing, man must have knowledge of his own being, and it cannot be said that humanity in general has yet advanced very far in this respect.

What is particularly characteristic of the present day? There is no shortage of ideals and programmes for the good of humanity. Practically every single individual comes forward as a small-scale Messiah and is anxious to create a picture of ideal human happiness. Above all there is no shortage of associations and societies founded for the purpose of introducing into our culture something they consider essential. There is also abundant faith in these programmes and ideals: indeed so convinced of their value are their promoters that it will soon be necessary to set up a kind of Council to establish the infallibility of individuals concerned! All this is deeply characteristic of our age.

Spiritual Science does not stop us from thinking about our future, but indicates certain fundamental laws and conditions which cannot be disregarded with impunity if its impulses are to achieve any positive effect. What does a modern man believe? An ideal takes shape in his soul and he considers himself capable of making it everywhere a reality. He does not pause to reflect that the time may not be ripe for its fulfilment, that the picture he has formed of it may be a caricature or that it can become mature only in a more or less distant future. In short, it is very difficult for a man to-day to understand that every event must be prepared for and occur at a particular point of time determined by macrocosmic conditions. Nevertheless this is a universal law and holds good for each individual as well as for the whole human race. We can recognise how this law affects an individual when we study his life in the light of Spiritual Science for we can turn to experiences lying very near at hand.

I am not going just to generalise but will keep to what can be observed. Let us suppose that someone conceives an idea which fires him with enthusiasm; it takes definite form in his soul and he is anxious to bring it in some way to fulfilment. The idea comes into his head and his heart urges him to act. In such circumstances a man of to-day will find it almost impossible to wait; he will go all out to bring this idea to fulfilment. Let us suppose that the idea is, in itself, insignificant, or merely a matter of information about scientific or artistic facts. An occultist, who knows the law, will not immediately proclaim his unfamiliar idea to the world. An occultist knows that such ideas live, first of all, in the astral body: the presence of enthusiasm in the soul is sufficient evidence of this, for enthusiasm is preeminently a force in the astral body. Now as a rule it will be harmful if at this stage a man does not let the idea rest as it is but proclaims it at once to his fellow-men or to the world, for the idea must follow a quite definite course. It must take deeper and deeper hold of the astral body and then impress itself into the etheric body like the imprint of a seal. If the idea is of no great importance this process may take seven days—that is the minimum time necessary. And if a man storms around with his idea he is always apt to overlook something very important, namely that after seven days there will be a subtle but quite definite experience. This experience we may have if we pay proper attention. But if a man rushes wildly around trying to launch the idea into the world, the soul will certainly not be alert to what may happen on the seventh day. In the case of an idea of only slight importance we shall always find that on the seventh day we don't really know what to do with it, and it fades away. We may feel ill at ease, perhaps inwardly worried and oppressed with all kinds of doubts, yet in spite of this we find ourselves attuned to the idea. Enthusiasm has changed into an intimate feeling of love: the idea is now in the etheric body.

If the idea is to continue to thrive it must now lay hold of the outer astral substance which always surrounds us. Hence it must pass from the astral body into the etheric body and from there into the outer astrality. For this, seven more days are needed. And unless the man in question is such a novice that when the idea begins to worry him he wants to get rid of it, he will realise, if he pays attention to what happens, that after this period something from without comes to meet his idea; he then recognises that it has been beneficial to wait fourteen days, because now he is not alone with his idea. It is as if he had been inspired from the Macrocosm, as if something had penetrated into his idea from the outer world. He will then for the first time feel in harmony with the whole spiritual world and will realise that it brings something to him when he has something to bring to it. A certain feeling of contentment arises after a period of about twice seven days.

But now the idea has to retrace its path, to pass from the outer astrality back into the etheric body. It has then become concrete and the temptation to communicate it to the world is very great. We must resist this with all our might, for there is now the danger that because the idea still lies in the etheric body, it may pass coldly into the world. If we wait another seven days the coldness leaves it and it is again filled with the warmth of the individual astral body and takes on a personal quality. That to which we gave birth and have allowed to be baptised by the Gods may now be given over to the world as our own. Every impulse in the soul must pass through these last three stages before it becomes fully mature. This holds good for ideas of no great significance.

In the case of an idea of weight and importance, longer periods will be necessary, but always in this rhythm of seven to seven.

You see, then, that what really matters is not, as a modern man thinks, to have an impulse in his soul but to be able to bear this impulse with patience, to let it be baptised by the World-Spirit and to let it live and achieve a state of maturity. Other such laws could be cited for the soul's development is a process full of ordered rhythms. For example, on some particular day—and such days vary greatly—we may feel that we have been blessed by the World-Spirit and ideas surge up from within us. In these circumstances it is a good thing not to lose our head but to recognise that after nineteen days a similar process of fructification may be expected. As I say, the development of the human soul is a process full of regular rhythms. On the whole, man has a healthy instinct not to carry these things to excess or to disregard them entirely. He takes heed of them, especially if he is one who aims at developing higher qualities and who allows them to mature; he heeds these things without being consciously aware of the law. It would be easy to show that in the creative work of artists there is evidence of a certain periodicity, a certain rhythmic process, a rhythm of days or weeks or years. This is particularly apparent in the lives of artists of the first rank—in the life of Goethe, for instance. It can easily be shown that something arises in Goethe's soul, becomes mature only after a period of four times seven years, and then appears in a different form.

In line with the tendency of the times, the general attitude might be: Yes, that is all very well; there may be such laws, but why should people trouble much about them? They will observe them instinctively.—Now that may have been true in the past; but because men are becoming more independent, more and more attentive to their own individuality, they must also learn to develop an inner calendar. Just as there are outer calendars of importance for everyday matters, so in the future, as the intensity of man's soul-life increases, he will have a feeling of 'inner weeks', of an inner ebb and flow of life, of inner 'Sundays', for the trend of humanity is towards an increasing inwardness. As we move towards the future, much of what man has experienced in the past as a result of the rhythmical periodicity of his life will be experienced later on as a macrocosmic resurrection in the life of soul. It will then seem to be an obvious duty to avoid bringing tumult and disorder into evolution by constantly transgressing the laws of the soul's development. Men will come to realise that the wish to communicate immediately whatever takes root in the soul is only a subtler form of egoism. They will come to feel the spirit working in the soul, not abstractly, as nowadays, but in conformity with law. And when some idea occurs to them, when they may desire to communicate some inner experience to others, they will not set about their fellow-men like raging bulls but listen to what spirit-filled nature has to say in their inmost soul.

What will it mean for men when they come more and more to recognise the spirituality which works in the world in obedience to law and by which they should let themselves be inspired? The vast majority of men to-day still have no feeling for such things. They do not believe that spiritual beings will lay hold of and work within their soul according to law. Even those who sincerely desire to work for cultural progress will for a long time yet regard it as madness to speak of this ordered activity of the spirit. And owing to the antipathy that is so prevalent to-day, those whose belief in the spirit is founded on spiritual-scientific knowledge will find that certain words in St. Mark's Gospel are directly applicable to them, and indeed to the present time:

> 'But when they shall lead you, and deliver you up, take no thought beforehand what ye shall speak, neither do ye premeditate: but whatsoever shall be given you in that hour, that speak ye; for it is not ye that speak, but the Holy Ghost' (xiii, 11).

We must try to understand a passage such as this, which has special significance for our own time because of its place in the whole framework not only of St. Mark's Gospel but in that of the other Gospels as well. Generally speaking, St. Mark's Gospel contains a good deal that is also found in the other Gospels. But there is one very remarkable passage which does not occur in the other Gospels and is particularly noteworthy because of the silly statements that have been made about it by biblical commentators. It is the passage where we are told that after Christ Jesus had chosen His disciples, He went out to preach to the people:

> 'And they went into an house. And the multitude cometh together again, so that they could not so much as eat bread. And when his friends heard of it, they went out to lay hold on him, for, they said, he is beside himself' (iii, 20–1).

When we consider that in the future course of human

evolution St. Paul's saying, 'Not I, but Christ in me', will become more and more true, that only an Ego which receives into itself the Christ Impulse can work fruitfully, we are justified in regarding the passage as particularly relevant to the present time. The destiny lived through by Christ Jesus during the events in Palestine will be lived through by the whole of mankind in the course of the ages. In the immediate future it will be more and more noticeable that wherever Christ is proclaimed with inner understanding, intense antipathy will be displayed by those who instinctively avoid Spiritual Science. It will not be difficult in the future to see how a prototypal event in Christ's life described in St. Mark's Gospel is coming to expression. Men's attitude to daily life, or the way in which art develops, and more particularly what is so widely accepted as science, will make it clear that what was said of Christ will be said of those who proclaim the Spirit in the truly Christian sense: There are many among them who seem to be beside themselves.

Again and again we must repeat that as time goes on the most important facts of the spiritual life as presented by Spiritual Science will be regarded as fantastic nonsense by the greater part of humanity. And from the Gospel of St. Mark we should draw the strength we need to stand firm in face of opposition to the truths that will be unveiled in the domain of the spirit.

If we have any feeling for the finer variations of style between the Gospel of St. Mark and the other Gospels, we shall also notice that the form in which certain things are presented by St. Mark is different from that to be found in the other Gospels. We become aware that through the actual structure of the sentences, through the omission of certain sentences found in the other Gospels, many things that might easily be taken abstractly are given definite shades of meaning. If we are sufficiently perceptive we shall realise that St. Mark's Gospel contains incisive and very important teaching concerning the 'I', concerning the inmost significance of the 'I' in man. To understand this we need only

look carefully at one passage in the Gospel which has all
the peculiar features due to the omission of details that are
included in the accounts given in the other Gospels. Here is
the passage in St. Mark's Gospel which, if there is a feeling
for such details, will indicate its deep significance:

> And Jesus went out accompanied by His disciples into the
> towns that are in the neighbourhood of Caesarea Philippi.
> And on the way He asked those who were around Him:
> 'What do men say of the 'I'? Whom do men recognise as
> the 'I'?'—And those who were around Jesus answered:
> 'Men say that in the 'I', if the 'I' is the true 'I', there must
> live John the Baptist; but others say that this 'I' must be
> filled with Elias, that Elias must live in the 'I'; others
> again say that another of the prophets must be regarded in
> such a way that the 'I' says: Not I, but this prophet
> works in me.' But He said to those around him: 'But
> whom do you say is the 'I'?' And Peter answered: 'We
> understand the 'I' in its essential spirituality to be Thou,
> the Christ!' And Christ charged those around Him: 'Tell
> nothing of this to ordinary men, for they cannot yet un-
> derstand this mystery!'

(viii, 27–33)*

But to those around Him who had been inwardly stirred by
His words He began to give this teaching:

> That which is the outward, physical expression of Ego-
> hood in the human being must endure much suffering if
> the 'I' is to live in man. The ancient Masters of humanity
> and those who have knowledge of the holiest wisdom
> declare that in the form in which the 'I' is present,
> it cannot function; in this form it must be killed and after a
> rhythm of three days—a rhythm determined by cosmic
> laws—it must rise again in a higher form. And they were

* Dr. Steiner was not quoting any of the usual versions of this
passage but giving an extended paraphrase to clarify the
points he wanted to make.

all amazed that He spoke these words openly before all men . . .

At this point I must make a comment. Up to that time such words would have been permissible only in the secrecy of the Mysteries. A secret otherwise strictly guarded in the Mystery-temples was that in the process of Initiation a man must pass through the experience of 'dying and becoming' and waken after three days. This is an indication of the meaning of the verses which are to the following effect.—

> Peter was amazed, took the Christ apart and intimated to Him that such things should not be spoken of openly. Then Christ Jesus turned about and said: 'In speaking thus, Peter, the words are being put into your mouth by Satan. The way in which you speak of this truth now belongs to the past, not to the present. In the past, such a truth was confined to the Temples; but in the future, because of the Mystery of Golgotha, it will be openly announced to all humanity. This is ordained by the divine guidance of world-evolution. Anyone who speaks in a contrary sense is not speaking out of divine wisdom but is distorting the divine wisdom into the form that was fitting only in the past.'

This is more or less how we must understand the above passage in the Gospel of St. Mark. We must realise that according to this Gospel the Christ Impulse means that we are to receive the Christ into the 'I', thus fulfilling the words of St. Paul, 'Not I, but Christ in me'—not an abstract Christ but the Christ who sent the Holy Spirit, the Spirit who works as inspiration in the human soul as described to-day, following the rhythms of an inner calendar.

In pre-Christian times these truths were accessible only to those who were initiated in the Mysteries and had remained for three and a half days in a deathlike condition, after having undergone the tragic sufferings which man must experience on the physical plane if he is finally to attain the heights of spiritual life. Such individuals learnt that the 'earthly man' must be discarded and slain, that a higher man must rise from within. This was the experience of 'dying and becoming'. What could formerly be experienced only in the Mysteries became historical fact through the Mystery of Golgotha, as I have shown in *Christianity as Mystical Fact*. Henceforward it was possible for all men who felt themselves united with the Mystery of Golgotha to become disciples of this great wisdom. Contemplation of what took place on Golgotha could now lead to an experience that could hitherto have been undergone only in the Mysteries. An understanding of the Christ Impulse is consequently the most important thing which a man can acquire for his earthly being, for the power which, since the coming of the Christ Impulse, must waken in the human 'I'.

In this present age we can be inspired in a special way by the Gospels. The Gospel of St. Matthew was a particularly valuable source of inspiration for the epoch in which the Christ Event actually occurred. For our own time the same can be said of the Gospel of St. Mark. We know that this is the age of the development of the Consciousness or Spiritual Soul which detaches itself, isolates itself, from its environment. We know too that in our age primary attention should not be paid to racial descent but rather to the living impulse expressed in the words of St. Paul: Not I, but Christ in me.

Our own fifth post-Atlantean epoch can, as I have said, be inspired particularly by the Gospel of St. Mark. By contrast, man's task in the sixth epoch will be to permeate himself wholly with the Christ Being. Whereas in the fifth epoch the Christ Being will be a subject of study, of deep meditation, in the sixth epoch men will be permeated by the Christ Being in all reality. They will find particular help in the Gospel of St. Luke, which reveals the whole origin of Jesus of Nazareth —that is to say, of the Jesus described in St. Matthew's Gospel who leads back to Zarathustra, and the Jesus of St. Luke's Gospel who leads back to the Buddha and Buddhism.

St. Luke's Gospel gives a picture of the evolution of Jesus of Nazareth, reaching back to the divine-spiritual origin of man. It will be more and more possible for man to feel himself a divine-spiritual being. To be permeated by the Christ Impulse can hover as an ideal before him but this ideal becomes reality only if, in the light of St. Luke's Gospel, he recognises physical man in the sense-world as a spiritual being having a divine origin.

The Gospel of St. John which may well be a manual of guidance for the spiritual life of man to-day will be the book of inspiration for the seventh post-Atlantean epoch. Men will then stand in need of a great deal which, as spiritual beings, they will have had to master during the sixth epoch. But they will also have to unlearn from its very foundations much of what they believe to-day. Admittedly, this will not be so very difficult because scientific facts will themselves show that many beliefs will have to be discarded.

To-day, for instance, a man would be considered to be 'out of his mind' if he were to maintain that the usual distinction made between 'motor' and 'sensory' nerves is nonsense. Motor nerves, as they are called, simply do not exist; there are only sensory nerves. The so-called motor nerves are sensory nerves, but their function is to make us aware of the corresponding movements in the muscles. Before very long it will be recognised that the muscles are not set in motion by the nerves but by the astral body—moreover by a force in the astral body that is not directly perceived in its real form: for it is a law that what is to produce an effect is not directly perceptible. What gives rise to movement in the muscles is connected with the astral body, in which a sound or tone, a kind of resonance, is produced. Something akin to music pervades the astral body and muscular movement is the expression of this. What happens can be compared with the well-known Chladni sound-figures which are produced when a fine powder or sand is scattered on a metal plate and forms itself into figures when the plate is made to vibrate by drawing a violin bow across it. Our astral body is filled with numbers of such figures or tone-forms which bring it into a particular condition. In a quite simple way you can convince yourself of this by tightening the biceps—the upper-arm muscle—and holding it close to your ear. When you have acquired the knack of making the muscle sufficiently taut and lay your thumb on it you will be able to hear a sound.— This is not meant to be taken as absolute proof but is merely a trivial illustration. We are, so to speak, permeated with music and give expression to this in the movements of our muscles. And we have the 'motor' nerves, as they are wrongly called, in order that we may be aware to some extent of the muscular movements. The way in which facts are grouped together in physiology still seems—but only seems—to contradict this.

This is one example of the kind of truths by which people will gradually be convinced that man is indeed a spiritual being, woven into the harmony of the spheres even in his muscles. And Spiritual Science which has to make preparation for a spiritual understanding of the world in the sixth post-Atlantean epoch, will have to concern itself in every detail with the truth that man is a spiritual being. Just as a musical tone rises into a higher sphere when it becomes a spoken human word, so in macrocosmic existence the harmony of the spheres rises to a higher stage when it becomes the Cosmic Word, the Logos.

Now in man's physical organism, the blood, in the physiological sense, is at a higher stage than the muscles. And just as the muscles are attuned to the harmony of the spheres, so is the blood attuned to the Logos and can be experienced more and more strongly as an expression of the Logos—as indeed has been the case unconsciously ever since man was created. This means that on the physical plane man will eventually feel the blood, which is the expression of the 'I', to be the expression of the Logos. And in the sixth epoch, when men have learnt to recognise themselves as spiritual beings, they will no longer cling to the fantastic idea that the muscles are moved by 'motor' nerves but will recognise that they are moved by the harmony of the spheres which has become part of their own personality.

In the seventh post-Atlantean epoch men will feel their very blood to be permeated by the Logos and will grasp for the first time the real content of what is said in St. John's Gospel. For not until the seventh epoch will the scientific nature of this Gospel come to be recognised. And then it will be felt that the first words of the Gospel ought to stand at the beginning of every book on physiology, that the whole of science should move in the direction indicated by these words. The best thing to say at the moment is that much of this can even to-day be understood, but by no means all; it can hover as an ideal before us.

Everything I have been saying indicates that St. Matthew's Gospel could be a source of inspiration especially for the fourth post-Atlantean epoch, just as that of St. Mark can be for our own. The Gospel of St. Luke will be especially important for the sixth epoch. We must ourselves prepare the conditions that will then prevail, for the seed of whatever the future holds in store must have been planted in the past. If we understand the contents of St. John's Gospel we shall find everything that is to be lived out in the further course of human evolution, everything that is to develop in the seventh epoch up to the time of the next great catastrophe. Therefore it will be particularly important for us to regard St. Mark's Gospel as a book that can give guidance for much that we must practise and also for much that we must guard against. The very sentences of this Gospel are themselves an indication of the significance of the Christ Impulse for the 'I' of man.

It is important to realise that our task is to grasp the reality of Christ in the spirit and to be aware of how Christ will reveal himself in future epochs. In my Rosicrucian Mystery Play, *The Portal of Initiation,* an attempt was made to indicate this task by words spoken by the seeress, Theodora. There will be something like a repetition of the event experienced by Paul at the gate of Damascus, but to believe that the Christ Impulse will come into the world again in a human physical body would merely be an expression of the materialism of our times. We can learn from the Gospel of St. Mark how to guard against such a belief, for the Gospel contains a special warning for our own epoch. And although much of the Gospel has a bearing on the past, its verses apply, in the high moral sense I have indicated, to our immediate future. We shall then realise the urgent necessity of the influence that must proceed from Spiritual Science.

If we understand the spiritual meaning of the following passage we shall be able to relate it to our own times and to the immediate future:

> 'For in those days shall be affliction, such as was not from the beginning of the creation which God created unto this time, neither shall be again' (xiii, 19–23).

These words must be applied to man's power of understanding. There is every prospect of affliction in the future, when truth will come to expression in its full spiritual reality.

> 'And except that the Lord had shortened those days, no flesh should be saved (that is to say, nothing would have been saved of spiritual nourishment): but for the elect's sake, whom he hath chosen, he hath shortened the days.'

Then come the words:

> 'And then, if any man shall say to you, Lo, here is Christ! or lo, he is there! believe him not. . . .'

Here the Gospel of St. Mark is pointing to a possible materialistic conception of Christ.

> 'For false Christs and false prophets shall rise, and shall show signs and wonders, to seduce, if it were possible, even the elect. But take ye heed: behold, I have foretold you all things!'

So powerful will be the onslaught of materialism that it will be essential for human souls to acquire the strength to stand the test expressed in the words: False Christs and false prophets will arise.—But if it is then said: Here is Christ!—those who have felt the true influence of Spiritual Science will obey the exhortation: If any man shall say to you, Lo, here is Christ—believe it not!

THE MOON-RELIGION OF JAHVE AND ITS REFLECTION IN ARABISM
THE PENETRATION OF THE BUDDHA-MERCURY STREAM INTO ROSICRUCIANISM

Today we shall be bringing to a close for the time being this winter's rather disconnected studies of St. Mark's Gospel. The passages quoted in the last lecture, to the effect that we are living in a period of transition are the key to the ideas with which we have been particularly concerned. On even a superficial consideration of spiritual life we must admit that thoughts and ideas of a new kind are emerging, although individuals living in the very midst of this new order hardly realise it themselves. It will be a good thing if we can take away material for thought which will help us to carry our ideas further, so this evening I want to give certain suggestions which will enable you to elaborate the spiritual-scientific knowledge already communicated to you.

When we refer to a period of transition it is well to remind ourselves of the greater epochs of transition in the evolution of humanity and particularly of the crucial point reached in the events in Palestine. From much that has been said we know the significance of that time. When we try to form some conception of how the supremely important idea, the Christ-idea, arose out of thoughts and feelings of the immediately preceding period, we must remember that the Jahve- or Jehovah-idea meant as much to the ancient Hebrews as the Christ-idea meant to those who became His followers. From other lectures we also know that for those who penetrate deeply into the essence of Christianity, the Being Jahve or Jehovah is not to be distinguished from Christ Himself. We must clearly understand that there is an intimate relationship between the Jahve-idea and the Christ-idea. It is difficult to summarise in a few words the vast aspects of the relationship. The subject has been elaborated in many lectures and lecture-courses in recent years, but I can illustrate it by a picture. I need only remind you again of the picture of the sunlight which can come to us either direct from the Sun or by reflection at night from the Moon, especially at Full Moon. After all, it is sunlight that comes from the Full Moon, even if it is reflected sunlight and this does indeed differ from sunlight directly received. If we think of Christ as symbolised by the direct sunlight, we may liken Jahve to sunlight reflected by the Moon and that would represent the exact sense in which the two ideas should be understood. Those who are to some extent conversant with this subject regard the transition from a temporary reflection of Christ in Jahve into Christ Himself just as they think of the difference between sunlight and moonlight: Jahve is an indirect and Christ a direct revelation of the same Being. Thinking in terms of evolution, however, we must picture what is side by side in space as *successive* in time. Those who speak of these things from the point of view of occultism will say: If we call the religion of Christ a Sun-religion—and there are good grounds for this expression if we recall what was said about Zarathustra—we may call the Jahve-religion a Moon-religion—the transitory reflection of the Christ-religion. Thus in the period preceding the birth of Christianity the Sun-religion was prepared for by a Moon-religion. You will only be able to understand what I am now going to say if you realise that symbols are not chosen arbitrarily but have deep foundations. When a world-conception or world-religion is associated with a symbol, those who use the symbol with adequate knowledge are aware that it is intimately and essentially connected with what it represents. People to-day have in many ways lost sight of the symbol of moonlight for the old Jahve-religion and to some extent also of the symbol of the Sun for Christianity.

You will remember how I have described the course of the evolution of humanity. First it is a descent, beginning when man was driven out of the spiritual world and sank more and more deeply into matter. And if we picture the general path of evolution, we can think of the lowest point as having been reached at the time of the Christ Impulse, after which the descent was transformed gradually into an ascent. The Christ Impulse began to have its effect at the lowest point and will continue to work until the Earth has achieved its mission.

Now evolution is a very complicated process and certain aspects of it are continuations of impulses given in earlier times. The Christ Impulse given at the beginning of our era will go straight forward, becoming more and more powerful in the souls of men until the goal of human evolution is reached—when from the souls of men it will influence the whole of life on the Earth. All later history will be evidence of the development and influence of this Impulse at a higher and more perfect stage. Many such impulses work in the world in the same way.

But there are also other impulses and factors in evolution which cannot be said to advance in a straight line. Some of them have already been mentioned. In post-Atlantean evolution we have distinguished seven epochs: the Old Indian, then in sequence, the Old Persian, the Egypto-Chaldean, the Graeco-Latin—during which the Christ event took place—and our own fifth epoch which will be followed by two others. In the fifth epoch, certain happenings characteristic of the Egypto-Chaldean epoch are repeated in a different form. The Christ Impulse was given in the middle epoch (the fourth) and the third epoch is in a certain sense repeated in the fifth. There is a similar relationship between the sixth and second epochs and between the seventh and first. Here we are concerned with overlapping factors of evolution which will reveal themselves in such a way that we can apply to them the Biblical saying: The first shall be last. The Old Indian epoch will reappear in the seventh in a different but nevertheless recognisable form.

There is, however, still another way in which an earlier epoch may have an effect in a later one. Shorter periods may also occur in the course of evolution. Thus conditions present in pre-Christian times during the period of ancient Hebrew culture reappeared later in post-Christian times: something that was prepared within the Jahve-or Jehovah-religion, overlapping the Christ Impulse as it were, appeared again and played into the other factors which had by then developed.

If, then, we try to describe by means of a symbol what pressure of time prevents our discussing adequately to-day, we may say: Taking the Moon, contrasted with the Sun, as the symbol representing the Jahve-religion, we may expect that a similar form of belief, by-passing as it were the Christ Impulse, would emerge later on as a kind of Moon-religion. And this is what actually happened. The old Jahve-religion emerged again after the Christ Event, in the religion of the Crescent, carrying earlier impulses into post-Christian times. If you do not take things superficially, the use of the Moon and Crescent as symbols for these two faiths will not be something to smile at, for it is an actual fact that a religion or creed and its symbol are intimately connected. So in a later time we have the repetition of an earlier phase which has skipped the intervening years. This takes place in the last third of the Graeco-Latin epoch which in the occult sense we reckon as lasting up to the twelfth and into the thirteenth century. Leaving out a period of six hundred years, this means that beginning in the sixth century A.D. and exercising a very vigorous influence upon all aspects of development, we have the religion brought by the Arabians from Africa over into Spain: this represents a re-emergence, in a different form, of the Jahve-Moon-religion. The intervening Christ Impulse has been ignored. It is not possible to enumerate all the characteristics brought over with the religion of Mohammed; but it is important to realise that the Christ Impulse is disregarded in the religion of Islam which was actually a kind of revival of Mosaic monotheism. This idea of the One God, however, included a good deal derived from other sources, for instance from Egypto-Chaldean religion, which had yielded very exact knowledge of the connection of happenings in the starry heavens with earthly events. Thus the thoughts and ideas current among the Egyptians, Chaldeans, Babylonians and Assyrians appear again in the religion of Mohammed but pervaded by the One God, Jahve. Speaking scientifically, what we have in Arabism is a kind of gathering-together, a synthesis, of the wisdom-teachings of the priests of Egypt and Chaldea and the Jahve-religion of the ancient Hebrews.

In such a process there is not only compression but also rejection and elimination. In this case everything connected with clairvoyant perception had to be discarded and men were to depend entirely upon reason and intellectual thinking. Hence the concepts belonging to the Egyptian art of healing and to Chaldean astronomy—which in both these peoples were the outcome of clairvoyance—are to be found in the Arabism of Mohammed in an intellectualised and individualised form. Something that had passed as it were through a filter was thus brought into Europe by the Arabians. Old concepts that had been current among the Egyptians and Chaldeans were denuded of their visionary, pictorial content and re-cast into abstract forms. They reappear in the wonderful scientific knowledge possessed by the Arabians who made their way into Europe via Africa and Spain. Whereas Christianity brought an impulse connected essentially with man's life of soul, the greatest impulse given to the human intellect was brought by the Arabians. Without thorough knowledge of the course taken by the evolution of humanity it is impossible to form any idea of how much the world-conception which arose in a new form under the symbol of the Moon, has given to mankind. There could have been no Kepler, no Galileo, without the impulses brought by Arabism into Europe. For the old mode of thinking appears again, but now denuded of its ancient clair-voyance, when the third culture-epoch celebrated its resur-rection in our own fifth epoch, in our modern astronomy, in our modern science.

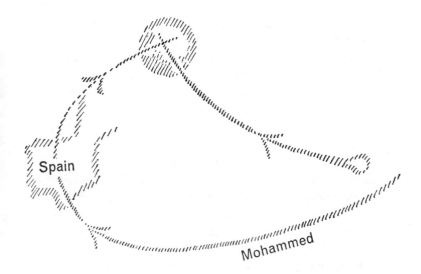

Thus the course of evolution is such that on the one hand the Christ Impulse penetrates into the European peoples directly, through Greece and Italy, and on the other hand a more southerly stream by-passes Greece and Italy and unites with the influences brought indirectly by the Arabians.

Only through the union of Christianity and Moham-medanism during the important period with which we are dealing, was it possible for our modern culture to come into being. For reasons which I cannot go into to-day we have to reckon with periods of six to six-and-a-half centuries for such impulses as I have been describing. Thus actually six cen-turies after the Christ Event the renewed Moon-cult of the Arabians appears, expanding and spreading into Europe, and until the thirteenth century enriching the Christian culture which had received its direct impulses by other paths. There was an unbroken interchange of thought. If you are conversant merely with the outer course of events, if you know how in the monasteries of Western Europe—in spite of apparent opposition to Arabism—the Arabian concepts made their way into science, you will also be aware that until the middle of the thirteenth century—again a particularly significant point of time—the Arabian impulse and the direct Christ Impulse were interwoven.

From this you will gather that the direct Christ Impulse actually moved along paths different from those taken by the impulses which streamed in like tributaries to unite with it. Six centuries after the Christ Event, as a result of happenings that are not easy to characterise although they are well known to every occultist, a new wave of culture arose in the East, made its way via Africa and Spain into the spiritual life of Europe and united with the Christ Impulse which had taken different paths. We can therefore say that the Sun-and-Moon-symbols merged into each other from the sixth/ seventh century up to the twelfth/thirteenth century—again a period of some six hundred years.

After this process of cross-fertilisation had in a certain respect achieved its goal, something new arose which had been in preparation since about the twelfth or thirteenth century. It is interesting that to-day even orthodox science recognises that something inexplicable passed through the souls of Europeans at that time. Science considers it inexplicable but occultism knows that in this period, as though it were following the Christ Impulse, something yielded by the fourth post-Atlantean epoch poured, spiritually, into the souls of men: the fruits of Greek culture constituted a following wave. We call this period the Renaissance—it was the culture which during the next centuries enriched everything already in existence. Here again there was an overlapping after a period of six hundred years since the influx of Arabism. At this point in evolution the age of Greece—which was a kind of centre among the seven post-Atlantean epochs—underwent a certain renewal in the Renaissance. Then again there is a period of six hundred

years, during which the Greek wave reaches ts culmination;
this brings us to the period in which we ourselves are living.
We are living to-day at the beginning of a period of transition
before the onset of the next six-hundred-year wave of culture, when something entirely new is pressing in upon us,
when the Christ Impulse is to be enriched by something new.
After the Moon-culture underwent its revival in the religion
symbolised by the Crescent and had reached its conclusion
during the period of the Renaissance, the time has now come
when the Christ Impulse must receive into itself another
tributary stream. With this tributary stream our own age has
a particular affinity. But we must clearly understand what
the influx of this new stream means to our own culture. All
these happenings are entirely in accordance with an occult
plan—we could also say, an occult purpose.

If we think of Moon, Mercury, Venus, Sun, in the old not
the new sequence, we should expect, after the renewal of the
Moon-influence had reached its culmination during the
Renaissance, the influx of another stream, to which we could
legitimately assign the symbol of Mercury. If our symbolism
is correct, just as we called the wave of Arabism a Moon-
culture, so we might say theoretically that we now face the
prospect of an influx of a form of Mercury-culture.

If we understand the way in which culture and civilisation
have developed we may justifiably name *Goethe* as the last
great individual to combine in his soul the full fruits of
science, (that is to say, intellectualism enriched by Arabism)
of Christianity and of Renaissance culture. We should
therefore expect him to represent a glorious union of the
three domains and having studied Goethe as we have been
doing for years we can easily recognise that these elements do
indeed flow together in his soul. But after what has been
said about the cycles of six hundred years we should not
expect to find in Goethe any trace of the Mercury-influence;
we should expect it to appear as something new only *after*
his time. And here it is interesting to note that Goethe's
pupil, Schopenhauer, already reveals signs of this new

influence. I have said that Schopenhauer's philosophy contains elements of Eastern wisdom, particularly in the form of Buddhism. Mercury has always been regarded as the symbol of Buddhism. So after the age of Goethe there was a revival of the Buddha-influence—Buddha standing for Mercury and Mercury for Buddha—in the same way as the Moon-influence reappeared in Arabism. This side-stream, which flowed into the direct Christ Impulse at the beginning of a new six-hundred-year period can therefore be described—within the limits indicated in my public lecture on the subject—as a revival of Buddhism.

We can now ask: Which is the stream of culture that flows straight forward into the future? It is the Christ-stream. And what side-streams are there? Firstly there is the Arabian stream which flows into the main current, then has a pause and finally passes into the culture of the Renaissance. At the present time a renewed influx of the Buddha-stream is taking place. If we are able to see these things in the right light it will become evident that we have to absorb those elements of the Buddha-stream which were not hitherto present in Western culture. And we can see how certain elements of the Buddha-stream are actually making their way into the spiritual development of the West, for instance, the teaching of Reincarnation and Karma. But there is something else that we must impress firmly upon our minds and it is this: none of these side-streams will ever be able to throw light on the central fact of our world-conception, of our Spiritual Science. To expect from Buddhism or any other pre-Christian oriental religion undergoing revival in our time any illumination on the nature of Christ would be no more intelligent than for European Christians to have expected this of the Arabians who had spread into Spain. The people of Europe at that time knew very well that the Christ-idea was foreign to the Arabians, that the Arabians could say nothing essential about the Christ. And when they did say anything the ideas put forward were incompatible with the true Christ-idea. The various prophets down to *Sabbatai*

*Zewi**, who appeared as false Messiahs without any understanding whatever of the Christ Impulse, all sprang from
Arabism. Obviously, therefore, the contribution of this
Arabian side-stream consisted of quite different elements; it
could shed no light on the central mystery of the Christ.

Our attitude to the stream that is approaching to-day as a
side-current must be the same. It is a revival of an older
stream and will promote understanding of Reincarnation and
Karma but cannot possibly bring any elucidation of the
Christ Impulse. That would be as absurd as if the Arabians,
although they were able to bring to Europeans many ideas
through false Messiahs up to the time of Sabbatai Zewi, had
set about giving Europe a true idea of Christ. Such occur-
rences will be repeated, for the evolution of mankind can go
forward only if men are strong enough to see through these
things with greater and greater clarity.

What we shall find is that the Spiritual Science founded by
European Rosicrucianism, with Christ as its central idea,
will establish itself despite external obstacles and penetrate
into the hearts of men in defiance of all temptations from
outside. From my book, *Occult Science,* you can gather how
the central Christ-idea must penetrate into human souls,
how the Christ is interwoven with the evolution not only of
humanity but of the whole world, and you will be able to
recognise along which path progress will be made. The
possibility of following this onward march of Spiritual
Science will be within reach of everyone who understands
the words from the Gospel of St. Mark quoted at the end of
the last lecture: 'False Christs and false prophets will
appear . . . when men say to you: 'Lo, here is the Christ, lo,
there!—believe them not!'—But beside this stream there is
another, claiming to be better informed than Western
Rosicrucian Spiritual Science about the nature of Christ.
This other stream will introduce all kinds of ideas and

* *Sabbatai Zewi* (1626–76), proclaimed himself publicly in the
year 1666 as the Messiah but subsequently became an adherent
of Islam.

dogmas which will develop quite naturally out of the side-stream of oriental Buddhism. But Western souls would be showing the worst kind of feebleness if they failed to understand that the Buddha- or Mercury-stream has as little light to throw on the direct development of the Christ-idea as Arabism had in its time. What I am saying now is not the outcome of any special belief, dogma or fantasy; it emerges from the objective course of world-evolution. If you wanted to follow this up I could prove by figures or by the trends of culture that things will inevitably be as occult science teaches.

But in connection with all this a distinction must be made. On the one hand there is orthodox oriental Buddhism in its original form. The attempt might be made to transplant this as a fixed and unalterable system into Europe and to produce out of it an idea, a conception, of Christ. On the other hand there is Buddhism that has progressed to further stages of development. There will be people who will tell you to think of the Buddha just as he was some five or six hundred years before our era and of the doctrines he then promulgated. But compare this with what Rosicrucian Spiritual Science has to say. It will say: The fault lies with you, not with the Buddha, that you talk as if Buddha had come to a standstill at the point he had attained all those centuries ago. Do you imagine that Buddha has not progressed? When you speak as you do, you are speaking of teaching that was right for his epoch. But we look to the Buddha who has moved onwards and from spiritual realms exercises an enduring influence upon human culture. We contemplate the Buddha as described in our studies of St. Luke's Gospel, whose influence streamed down upon the Jesus of the Nathan line of the House of David; we contemplate the Buddha at the further stage of his development in the realm of the spirit, who proclaims from there the truths of basic importance for our time.

Something strange has happened in dogmatic Christianity in the West. By a curious concatenation of circum-

stances a Buddha-like figure has appeared among the
Christian Saints. You will remember that I once spoke of a
legend current all over Europe in the Middle Ages, namely,
the legend of Barlaam and Josaphat. Its content was more or
less as follows.—There was once an Indian King who had a
son. In his early years, far removed from all human misery
and life in the outer world, the son was brought up in the
royal palace, where he saw only conditions making for
human happiness and well-being. Josaphat was his name,
though it has been frequently changed and has assumed
several different forms—Josaphat, Judasaph, Budasaph.
Until a certain age Josaphat lived in his father's palace,
knowing nothing about the world outside. Then one
day he was led out of the palace and came to know something of the world. First of all he saw a leper, then a blind
man, then an old man. Thereafter he met a Christian hermit
by the name of Barlaam, who converted him to Christianity.

You will not fail to recognise in this legend clear echoes of
the legend of Buddha. He too was an Indian king's son who
lived isolated from the world, was later led out of the palace
and saw a leper, a blind man and an old man. But you will
notice that in the Middle Ages something was added that
cannot be attributed to Buddha, namely that Josaphat
allowed himself to be converted to Christianity. This could
not have been said of Buddha. The legend evoked a certain
response among individual Christians, particularly among
those who were responsible for drawing up the calendar of
the Saints.

It was known that the name Josaphat, Judasaph, Budasaph, is directly connected with Bodhisattva. So here we
have evidence of a remarkable connection of a Christian
legend with the figure of Buddha. We know that according
to the Eastern legend Buddha passed into Nirvana, having
handed on the Bodhisattva's crown to his successor, who is
now a Bodhisattva and will subsequently become the
Maitreya Buddha of the future. Buddha is presented to us in

the legend in the figure of Josaphat; and the union of
Buddhism with Christianity is wonderfully indicated by the
fact that Josaphat is included among the Saints. Buddha
was held to be so holy that in the legend he was converted to
Christianity and from being the son of an Indian king could
rightly be included among the Saints—although from another
side this has been disputed.

From this you will see that it was known where the later
form of Buddhism, or rather of the Buddha, was to be sought.
In hidden worlds the union has meanwhile taken place
between Buddhism and Christianity. Barlaam is the mysterious figure who brings Christianity to the knowledge of the
Bodhisattva. Consequently if we trace the course of Buddhism
as an enduring stream in the sense indicated in the legend,
we can accept it only in the changed form in which it now
appears. If through clairvoyant insight we understand the
inspirations of the Buddha, we must speak of him as he
actually exists to-day. Just as Arabism was not Judaism and
the Jahve-Moon-religion did not reappear in Arabism in its
original form, neither will Buddhism—to the extent to which
it can enrich Western culture—appear in its old form. It
will appear in an altered form, because what comes later
never appears as a mere replica of the earlier.

These are brief, disconnected remarks intended to stimu-
late thought about the evolution of humanity, and you can
elaborate them for yourselves. If you will take everything you
can discover in the way of historical knowledge and follow
the development of Europe from the spiritual-scientific
point of view you will see clearly that we have now reached
the point where a fusion of Christianity and Buddhism will
take place, just as in the case of the Jahve-religion and
Christianity. Test this by whatever European historians can
tell you: but test it by taking *all* the facts into consideration.
You will then find confirmation of everything I have said,
although it would be necessary to talk for weeks if we were to
speak of all that the Rosicrucian Movement in Europe can
contribute.

Nor is it only in history that you can find proof of these things. If you set about it rightly you will find proof in modern natural science and allied fields. If you seek in the right way you will find that everywhere the new ideas are thrusting their way into the present; old ideas are becoming useless and are disappearing. In a certain respect our thinkers and investigators are working with outworn concepts because the great majority of them are incapable of assimilating ideas and concepts contributed by the new cultural side-stream, particularly on the subject of Reincarnation and Karma, as well as all the other contributions which Spiritual Science can make. Our scientists are working with concepts that have become useless. If you look through the literature of any field of science you will realise how heart-breaking it often is for scholars that current concepts are quite unable to elucidate the innumerable facts that are constantly coming to light.

There is one concept—I can only touch on these things to-day—which still plays an important part in the whole range of science: it is the concept of *heredity*. The concept of heredity as it figures in the different sciences and in common usage is simply useless. Facts themselves will force people to recognise the need for concepts other than the useless one of heredity as currently accepted in many fields of science. It will become evident that certain facts already known to-day in regard to the heredity of man and related creatures, can be understood only when quite different concepts are available. When speaking to-day of heredity in successive generations we seem to believe that all a man's faculties can be traced back in a direct line through his immediate ancestors. But it is the concept of Reincarnation and Karma alone that will make it possible for clarity to replace the present confusion in this field of thought. Again I cannot go into detail, but it will become evident that a great deal in human nature as we know it to-day is entirely unconnected with the influence of the sexes; nevertheless a confused science still teaches that everything in the human being originates at the time of conception, through the union of male and female. But it is simply not true that everything in the human being is in some way connected with what takes place in direct physical manifestation in the union of the sexes. You will have to think this out more closely for yourselves; I only want what I have said to be a suggestion.

Man's physical body, as you know, has a long history. It has passed through a Saturn period, a Sun period, a Moon period, and is now passing through the Earth period. The influence of the astral body began only during the Moon period but naturally produced a change in the physical body. Hence the physical body does not appear to us to-day in the form imparted to it by the forces of the Saturn epoch and the Sun epoch, but in the form resulting from those forces combined with the forces of the astral body and the 'I'. It is only those components of the physical body which are connected with the influence of the astral body on the physical body which can be inherited as the result of the union of the sexes whereas whatever in the physical body is subject to laws going back to the Saturn and Sun periods has nothing to do with the sexes. One part of man's nature is received directly from the Macrocosm and not from the union of the sexes. This means that what we bear within us does not all spring from the union of the sexes; only that which depends upon the astral body springs from that union. A large part therefore of our human nature is received—for example by way of the mother—directly from the Macrocosm and not by the roundabout way of union with the other sex.

We must therefore distinguish in man's nature one part that originates from the union of the sexes and another part that is received by way of the mother directly from the Macrocosm. There can be no clarity in these matters until a definite and precise distinction is made between the individual members of man's nature, whereas to-day everything is mingled together in confusion. The physical body is not a self-contained, isolated entity; it is formed through the combined workings of the etheric body, the astral body and the

'I'; and again we must distinguish between the forces that arc due to the direct influence of the Macrocosm and others that are to be ascribed to the union of the sexes.

But from the paternal organism too, something is received that again has nothing whatever to do with the union of the sexes. Certain laws and organs in no way based upon heredity are implanted direct from the Macrocosm through the maternal organism; others come from the Macrocosm by spiritual channels through the paternal organism. Of what is received by way of the maternal organism we may say that this organism is the focus through which it is transmitted; but this combines with something that again is not derived from sexual union but from the father. A macrocosmic process thus takes place and comes to expression in the bodily members and forms. Consequently when speaking of the development of the human embryo it is completely misleading to base everything upon heredity, when in actual fact certain elements are received direct from the Macrocosm.

Here, then, we have a case in our own times where the facts themselves far outstrip the concepts at the disposal of science, for these concepts originated in an earlier epoch. You may ask: Is there any evidence to confirm this? Popular literature has little to say, but occultism is absolutely clear about it. And here I should like to draw your attention to something, of which, however, I can give no more than a hint.—A remarkable contrast between two naturalists of the modern age has attracted widespread attention and has influenced other thinkers to a very considerable extent. The characters of the two naturalists are very relevant here. On the one side there is *Haeckel*. Because Haeckel applies ancient concepts to his really wonderful collection of facts and data, he traces everything to heredity and bases the whole development of the embryo upon it. On the other side there is *His*,* the zoologist and scientist, who keeps very closely to the facts as such and because of this might possibly

* Wilhelm His (1831–1904).

be accused, with a certain justification, of doing too little thinking. Because of the particular way in which he investigated his facts he was bound to oppose the concept of heredity as propounded by Haeckel and he pointed out that certain organs and organic structures in the human being can be explained only if the view that they originate from the union of the sexes, is discarded. To this Haeckel mockingly retorted that His was attributing the origin of the human being to a virginal influence independent of any sexual union! But as a matter of fact this is quite correct. Scientific facts more or less compel us to-day to admit that what can be attributed to the union of the sexes must be distinguished from what comes direct from the Macrocosm—which wide circles of people nowadays naturally regard as absurd. So you can see that even in the field of natural science we are being driven towards new concepts. The present phase of evolution makes it evident that to have a genuine grasp of the facts presented by science we must acquire many new concepts and that those inherited from past ages no longer suffice.

From what I have said you will realise that a tributary stream must flow into our present culture. This is the Mercury-stream, the existence of which proclaims itself in the fact that those undergoing occult development as described in many of our lectures, grow into the spiritual world and in so doing experience new facts and realities. This penetration into another world may be compared with the way in which a fish is transferred from water into the air but must first have prepared itself by turning its gills into lungs. Similarly, a man whose faculty of sense-perception is developing into spiritual perception will have made his soul capable of using certain forces in a different element. The very atmosphere nowadays is saturated with thoughts which make it necessary for us to have a genuine grasp of the new facts of science becoming evident on the physical plane. The spiritual investigator can penetrate into the real nature of the facts that press in upon him from all sides. This is due to the appearance of the new stream of which I have been speaking. Thus wherever we look, we find that we are living in an extraordinarily important epoch, in times when it will be impossible for life to progress unless revolutionary changes take place in men's thinking and perception.

I said that man must learn to live in a new element in the same way that a fish, accustomed to living in water, would have to find its way into the new element of air. But men must be able, in their thinking too, to penetrate to the real nature of the facts produced on the physical plane. If they stand out against this new thinking they will be in the same position as fish taken out of the water; later on they will literally be gasping for spiritual concepts. Those who want to retain the monism of to-day are like fish who might prefer to exchange their watery for an airy habitation, but at the same time want to keep their gills. Only those human souls who so transform their faculties that a new conception of present facts is within their reach will grasp what the future has in store.

So we find ourselves living, but now with full understanding, at a point where two streams converge. The first stream should give us a deeper understanding of the Christ-problem and the Mystery of Golgotha; the other should inaugurate new ideas and concepts of reality. The two streams must converge in our time. But this will not happen without great hindrances being encountered; for in periods when two such streams of thought and outlook converge, all kinds of obstructions arise. And in a certain sense it is the adherents of Spiritual Science who will find it particularly necessary to understand these facts.

Some of our members might counter the exposition I have been giving here, by saying: What you have told us is very difficult to understand and we shall have to work at it for a long time. Why do you not give us something more readily digested, which convinces us of the spirituality of the world and makes a greater appeal? Why do you expect so much of our understanding of the world? How much pleasanter it

would be if we could believe what a Buddhism transmitted
exactly as it was at the beginning, can tell us: that we need
not think of the Christ Event as the single point on which the
scales of world-evolution hinge and that there can be no
repetition of it. It would be so much easier to think that a
Being such as the Christ incarnates again and again like
other men. Why do you not say that here or there this
Being will come again in the flesh—instead of saying that
men must make themselves capable of experiencing a
renewal of what happened to St. Paul at the gate of Damascus? For if you told us that there will be an incarnation of the
Christ Being in the flesh, we could say: 'Behold, he is here!
We can see him with physical eyes!'—That would be so very
much easier to understand.

Plenty of people will see to it that this kind of thing is said.
But it is the mission of Western Spiritual Science to make
known the truth—the truth which takes full account of all
the factors responsible for the progress of evolution to this
day. Those who look for comfort and ease in the spiritual
world will have to seek for spirituality along other paths. The
truth needed for our times is that to which we must apply all
the intellectual capacity acquired since the fading of the old
clairvoyance; this must carry us on until the dawn of the
new clairvoyance. And I am sure that those who understand
the nature of this intellectual capacity in the form necessary
for to-day will follow the path indicated in the words I have
spoken here now, and so often before. It is not a matter of
saying in what form we wish to have the truth but of knowing
from the whole course of human evolution in a given epoch,
how, at a particular point of time, the truth must be proclaimed. You may be sure that plenty of other things will be
said, and you must not be unprepared for them. Consequently in Rosicrucian Spiritual Science we shall not fail to
draw attention again and again to the highest spiritual
knowledge attainable in our time. You need never accept
blindly on trust anything said here or elsewhere, for in our
Movement we never appeal to blind credulity. In your own

intelligence and the use of your own reason you have adequate means of testing what you hear. And remember, as you have been told so often, that you must bring the whole of life, the whole of science and the whole of your experience, to bear upon what you hear in Rosicrucian Spiritual Science. Do not fail to put everything to the test. It is precisely where you come across incongruities or perhaps where the truth seems to be the very opposite of what is stated, that on the ground of true spirituality blind faith cannot be allowed. Everything based on blind faith is bound to be sterile and stillborn. It would be easy enough to build on credulity: but those who belong to the stream of Western spiritual life refuse to do this. They build instead upon what can be tested by human reason, understanding and intellect. Those in touch with the source of our Rosicrucian Spiritual Science know that whatever is said has been carefully tested. The edifice of Spiritual Science is built upon the ground of truth, not upon that of easy faith; it is upon the foundation of a thoroughly tested, though perhaps difficult truth, that we establish our Spiritual Science; and prophets of a blind and comfortable faith will not shake that foundation.

ROSICRUCIAN WISDOM IN FOLK-MYTHOLOGY

There is no doubt that the Spiritual Science we have been studying for many years is beginning to make more and more headway in the world and to find increasing understanding in the hearts and minds of our contemporaries. It might be useful occasionally to speak of how the ideas of Spiritual Science are being made known and many of you would be glad to know what effect the spiritual nourishment you have yourselves received has had upon others at the present time. It is only now and then that I can speak of this spread of spiritual-scientific thought in the outer world, but it will be some satisfaction to you to know that we can see how the spirit inspiring us all is finding entry in various countries. I could see, for instance, that our ideas were beginning to find a footing when I was lecturing in the south of Austria, in Trieste, recently. Then, when I gave a course of lectures in Copenhagen* only a few days ago, there too it was evident that the spirit we are trying to cultivate under the symbol of the Rose Cross is gaining more and more ground. Signs such as these make it clear that there is a need and also a longing for what we call Spiritual Science.

It is fundamental to the spirit informing our Movement that we should refrain from any agitation or propaganda and far rather pay heed to the great, all-embracing wisdom needed by the hearts and souls of modern men if they are to feel any security in life to-day. It is our duty to make these spiritual thoughts into real nourishment for our souls. You will certainly have understood enough of the great law of Karma to know that it is by no chance or accident that an

* *The Spiritual Guidance of Man and of Mankind.* (Obtainable from Rudolf Steiner Press.)

individual feels urged to come down into the physical world
at this particular time. The souls of all of you here have felt
the longing to incarnate in a physical body at the turn of the
nineteenth to the twentieth century because of a desire to
experience what can be achieved in the present physical
environment.

Let us look at our own epoch and see how its spiritual
aspect appears to souls which, like yours, have been born into
it. At the turn of the century conditions were very different
from what they had been fifty or sixty years earlier. Human
beings who—like all of you here—are growing up at the
present time, attempt now and then to hear about the spiritual guidance and leadership of the world, about the
spiritual forces and influences pervading the external world
in the different kingdoms of nature and penetrating into the
souls of men. But for the last fifty years a soul longing and
searching for spiritual nourishment has found very little.
This longing has been present in the depths of men's souls,
although it may have been a very faint voice, easily silenced.
Nevertheless the longing is there and everyone is seeking for
spiritual nourishment, whatever his position in life and
whatever use he may make of his faculties. No matter in
what department of science you may be working to-day, you
learn only external, material facts; they can be utilised very
cleverly and ingeniously to advance modern culture but they
are no help at all towards understanding what the spirit may
reveal. No matter whether you are an artist or are engaged in
some practical work, you will find little that can pass into
head or hand to give you not only energy and impetus for
your work but also security and comfort in life. By the begin-
ing of the nineteenth century people had forebodings that in
the near future very little spiritual nourishment would be
left. During the first half of the century, when vestiges of an
old spiritual life were still present, although in a different
form, many people felt that there was something in the air
presaging the complete disappearance of the ancient treas-
ures of the spirit handed down by tradition from olden times.

Yet it is precisely the legitimate progress of culture during the nineteenth century that will completely wipe out the spiritual traditions handed down from the past.

During the first half of the nineteenth century, many voices are to be heard speaking in this strain and I will quote one example of a man who lived during that period and had a wide knowledge of the old form of theosophy, but who also knew that owing to the course of events in that century it was bound to disappear; at the same time he was convinced that a future must come when there would be a revival of this old theosophy but in a new form. I am going to read you a passage written towards the end of the first half of the nineteenth century, in 1847. Its author was a thinker of a type no longer in existence to-day—men who were still sensitive to the last echoes of those old traditions which have now been lost for a considerable time.—

'It is often difficult to learn among the older theosophists what the real purpose of theosophy is . . . but it is clear that along the paths it has taken hitherto, theosophy can acquire no real existence as a science nor achieve any result in a wider sphere. Yet it would be very ill-advised to conclude that it is a phenomenon scientifically unjustifiable and also ephemeral. History itself decisively disproves this: it shows how this enigmatic phenomenon could never make itself really effective in the world but for all that was continually breaking through and was held together in its manifold forms by the chain of a never-dying tradition. . . . At all times there have been very few in whom this insistent speculative need has been combined with a living religious need. But theosophy is for these few alone. . . . The important thing is that if theosophy ever becomes scientific in the real sense and produces obvious and definite results, these will gradually become the general conviction, be acknowledged as valid truths and be universally accepted by those who cannot find

their way along the only possible path by which they could
be discovered.

But all this lies in the womb of the future which we do not
wish to anticipate. For the moment let us be thankful for
the beautiful presentation given by Oetinger, which will
certainly be appreciated in wide circles.'

This shows what a man such as *Rothe* of Heidelberg felt
about the theosophical spirit in 1847. The passage is from his
Preface to a treatise on Oetinger, a theosophist living in the
second half of the eighteenth century.

What, then, can be said about the spirit of theosophy? It is
a spirit without which the genuine cultural achievements of
the world would never have been possible. Thinking of its
greatest manifestations, we shall say: Without it there would
never have been a Homer, a Pindar, a Raphael, a Michelangelo; there would have been no depth of religious feeling
in men, no truly spiritual life and no external culture.
Everything that man creates he must create from out of the
spirit. If he thinks that he can create without it he is ig-
norant of the fact that although in certain periods spiritual
striving falls into decline, the less firmly rooted a thing is in
the spirit the more likely it is to die. Whatever has eternal
value stems from the spirit and no created thing survives that
is not rooted in it. But since everything a man does is under
the guidance of the spiritual life, the very smallest creation,
even when used for the purposes of everyday life, has an
eternal value and connects him with the spirit. We know
that our own theosophical life has its source in what we have
called the Rosicrucian stream; and it has often been emphasised that since the eleventh, twelfth and thirteenth
centuries the Masters of Rosicrucian wisdom have been
preparing conditions that began at the end of the nineteenth
century and will continue in the twentieth. The future
longed for and expected by Rothe of Heidelberg is already
the present and should be recognised as such. But those who
caused this stream to flow into souls, at first in a way

imperceptible to men, have been preparing conditions for a long, long time. In a definite sense what we have called the Rosicrucian path since the twelfth, thirteenth and fourteenth centuries is present in our Theosophical Movement in a more conscious form; its influence has flowed into the hearts and minds of the peoples of Europe and sets its stamp upon them.

From what has happened in European culture, can we form an idea of how this spirit has actually taken effect? I said just now that it has worked as the true Rosicrucian spirit since the eleventh, twelfth, thirteenth and fourteenth centuries; it was always present although only at that time did it assume Rosicrucian form. This Rosicrucian spirit goes back to a very distant past—it had its Mysteries even in Atlantean times. The influence has been taking effect for long ages, becoming more and more conscious as it streamed into the hearts and souls of men.

Let us try to form some idea of how this spirit made its way into humanity. We meet together here and our studies help us to perceive ways in which the human soul develops and gradually rises to regions where it can understand the spiritual life, and perhaps actually behold it. Many of you have for years been trying to let concepts and ideas which mirror the spiritual life stream into your souls as spiritual nourishment. You know how we have tried to acquire some understanding of the riddles of the world. I have often described the different stages of the soul's development and how it can rise to the higher worlds; how a higher part of the Self must be distinguished from a lower part; how man has come from other planetary conditions, having passed through a Saturn-, a Sun- and a Moon-evolution, during which his physical, etheric and astral bodies were formed; and how finally he entered into the period of Earth-evolution. I have told you that there is something within us that must receive its training here on the Earth in order to rise to a higher stage. We have also said that the development of certain beings—the Luciferic beings—was retarded during

the Old Moon-period and they later approached man's
astral body as tempters, and also in order to impart to
him certain qualities. I have often told you too how man
must overcome certain tendencies in his lower self and
through this conquest rise into the spheres to which his
higher Self belongs, into the higher regions of the spiritual
life. Words of Goethe must be remembered:

> And as long as thou knowest it not,
> This Dying and Becoming,
> Thou art but a troubled guest
> Upon the dark Earth!

The degree of development that is possible to-day and can
give strength, assurance and a genuine content to life is
within our reach if we acquire knowledge of the manifold
nature of man and realise that his constitution is not a
haphazard medley but consists of physical body, etheric body,
astral body and Ego. We have formulated definite ideas, for
example of the temperaments, by studying the process of
education and the development of the physical body up to
the seventh year, of the etheric body up the fourteenth and
of the astral body up to the twenty-first year. By studying the
mission of Truth, of Prayer, of Anger, our ideas of the three
bodies, of the sentient soul, intellectual or mind-soul and
consciousness—or spiritual soul, do not remain mere abstractions but impart meaning, clarity and content to our existence.

In this way we have achieved some understanding of the
riddles of the world. And although there are large numbers of
people outside our circle who still, consciously or unconsciously, persist in materialism, there are nevertheless many
souls who feel it necessary to their very existence to listen to
expositions of the kind we have been able to give. Many of
you would not have been present among us for years, sharing
our experiences and activities if it were not a necessity of your
very lives. Why are there souls to-day who understand these
things and for whom the ideas and concepts developed here

become a guide on their life's way? The reason is this.—
Just as you have been born into the modern world with these
longings, so our forbears in Europe—and this means very
many of those present here to-day—were born during past
centuries into a world and environment very different from
those of the nineteenth century. Let us cast our minds back
to the sixth, seventh or even the twelfth and thirteenth
centuries of our era when many of those present here were
incarnated, and think of the sort of things that souls then
living might have experienced.

In those times there was no Theosophical Society where
subjects such as those with which we are concerned were
studied; the influence of the environment upon the souls of
men took a very different form. People did not travel about
giving lectures on spiritual-scientific subjects, but minstrels
went from village to village, from city to city, proclaiming
the spirit. These minstrels did not speak about theosophy,
about the lower and higher Ego, about man's physical,
etheric and astral bodies and so on. As they moved around
the land their mission was to speak of the spirit in the way it
was wont to be proclaimed at that time. The following
story was told all over Middle and Eastern Europe.—

Once upon a time there was a King's son. During a ride
one day he heard moans coming from a ditch, and following
the course of the ditch in order to discover the source of the
moans, he found an old woman. He dismounted, climbed
down into the ditch and helped the old woman who had
fallen into it, to get out. Then he saw that she had injured
her leg and could not walk. He asked her how the accident
happened and she told him: 'I am old and I have to get up
soon after midnight to go to the city and sell my eggs; on the
way I fell into this ditch.' The King's son said to her: 'You
cannot get home by yourself so I will put you on my horse
and take you.' This he did, and the woman said to him:
'Although you are of noble birth, you are a kind and good
man; and because you have helped me I will give you a
reward.' He guessed now that she was not an ordinary

woman, for she said: 'You shall have the reward which your kind soul has earned. Do you want to marry the Flower-Queen's daughter?' 'Yes!' he replied. She went on: 'For that you will need something that I can easily give you,' and she gave him a little bell, saying: 'If you ring this bell once the Eagle-King will come with his hosts to help you in the predicament in which you find yourself; if you ring twice the Fox-King will come with his hosts to help you in the predicament in which you find yourself; and if you ring three times the Fish-King will come with his hosts to help you in the predicament in which you find yourself.'—The King's son took the little bell and returned home, announced that he was going to search for the Flower-Queen's daughter, and rode off. He rode a long, long way but nobody could tell him where the Flower-Queen lived with her daughter. By this time his horse was completely exhausted and could carry him no longer so that he was obliged to continue his journey on foot. He came across an aged man and asked him where the Flower-Queen lived. 'I cannot tell you,' the aged man replied, 'but go on and on and you will find my father who may perhaps be able to tell you.' So the King's son went on, year after year, and then found another, still more aged man. He asked him: 'Can you tell me where the Flower-Queen lives?' But the aged man replied: 'I cannot tell you, but you must go on and on for many more long years and you will find my father who will certainly be able to tell you where the Flower-Queen lives.'—So the King's son went on and at last found an old, old man and asked him if he could tell him where the Flower-Queen lived with her daughter. The old man replied: 'The Flower-Queen lives far away, in a mountain which you can see from here in the distance. But she is guarded by a fearsome Dragon. You cannot get near at present for this is a time when the Dragon never sleeps; he sleeps at certain times only and this is one of his waking periods. But you must go a little further, to another mountain, and there you will find the Dragon's mother; through her you will attain your goal.' So he went on and found the Dragon-mother, the very archetype of ugliness. But he knew that whether he could find the Flower-Queen's daughter would depend on her. Then he saw seven other dragons around her, all eager to guard the Flower-Queen and her daughter who had been long imprisoned and were destined to be set free by the King's son. So he said to the Dragon-mother: 'I know that I must become your servant if I am to find the Flower-Queen.' 'Yes', she said, 'you must become my servant and perform a task that is not easy. Here is a horse which you must lead to pasture the first day, the second day and the third. If you can bring it home in good condition you may possibly achieve your object after three days. But if you fail, the dragons will devour you—we shall all devour you.' The King's son agreed to this and the next morning he was given the horse. He tried to lead it to pasture but it soon disappeared. He searched for it in vain and was in despair. Then he remembered the little bell given him by the old woman, took it out and rang it once. A host of eagles gathered, led by the Eagle-King, looked for the horse and found it, so that the King's son was able to take it back to the Dragon-mother. She said to him: 'Because you have brought the horse back I will give you a cloak of copper so that you can attend the Ball tonight at the court of the Flower-Queen and her daughter.' Then, on the second day, he was again given the horse to take to pasture, but again it disappeared and he could not find it. So he took out the bell and rang it twice. Immediately the Fox-King appeared with a host of his followers; they looked for and found the horse and the King's son was again able to take it back to the Dragon-mother. She then said to him: 'To-day you shall have a cloak of silver so that you can attend the Ball to-night at the court of the Flower-Queen and her daughter.' At the Ball the Flower-Queen said to him: 'On the third day ask for a foal of that horse and with it you will be able to rescue me and we shall be united.' Then, on the third day, the horse was again handed to him to lead to pasture, and again it soon disappeared, for it was very wild.

So he took out the bell and rang it three times, whereupon the Fish-King appeared with his followers, found the horse, and for the third time the King's son brought it home. He had now successfully performed his task. The Dragon-mother then presented him with a mantle of gold as his third garment in order that on the third day he might attend the Flower-Queen's Ball. He was also given as a fitting reward the foal of the horse he had cared for. With it he was able to lead the Flower-Queen and her daughter to their own castle. And around the castle, since there were others who wanted to steal her daughter, the Flower-Queen caused a thick hedge to grow to prevent the castle from being invaded. Then the Flower-Queen said to the King's son: 'You have won my daughter and henceforth she shall be yours, but only on one condition. You may keep her for half the year but for the other half she must return beneath the surface of the earth and be restored to me. Only on this condition can you be united with her.' So the King's son won the Flower-Queen's daughter and lived with her for half the year, while for the other half she was with her mother.—

This story, as well as others like it, was listened to by many people in those days. They listened and drank in what they heard but did not, like many modern theosophists, proceed to invent allegories, for symbolic or allegorical interpretations of such matters are valueless. People listened to the stories because they were a source of delight to them and a warm glow pervaded their souls as they listened. They wanted nothing more than this as they listened to the story of the Flower-Queen and the King's son with his bell and his wooing of the Flower-Queen's daughter.

There are many souls alive to-day who in those days heard such tales with inner delight, and the effects lived on in them. Their feelings and perceptions were converted into thoughts and experiences and their souls were transformed by new forces. These forces have changed into the longing for a higher interpretation of the same secrets, a longing for Spiritual Science. In those days the wandering minstrels did

not go about saying that man strives towards his higher self
and to that end must overcome his lower self which holds
him back. They gave their message in the form of a story
about a King's son who rode out into the world, heard
moans coming from a ditch and thereupon performed a good
deed. To-day we speak simply of a good deed, a deed of love
and sacrifice. In earlier times the deed was described in
pictures. To-day we say that man must develop a feeling for
the spirit which will awaken in him an inkling of the spiritual
world and create powers through which he can establish
relationship with it. In earlier times this was expressed in the
picture of the old woman who gave the King's son a bell
which he rang. To-day it is said: Man has taken into himself
all the kingdoms of nature and unites in harmony everything
that lies outspread before him. But he must learn to understand how what is outspread in the external world lives
within him and how he can overcome his lower nature, for
only if he can bring what is at work in the kingdoms of
nature into the right relationship with his own being can it
come to his aid.

We have spoken often enough of man's evolution through
the periods of Saturn, Sun and Moon and of how he left
behind him the other kingdoms of nature, retaining within
himself the best of each in order that he might rise to a
higher stage. To what stage has he evolved? To indicate
what lives in the human soul Plato had already used the
picture of the horse on which man rides from one incarnation
to another. In the times of which we have been speaking the
picture used was that of the bell which was rung to summon
the representatives of the kingdoms of nature—the Eagle-
King, the Fox-King and the Fish-King—in order that the
being destined to become the ruler of these kingdoms might
establish the right relationship with them.

Man's soul is unruly and can be brought into the right
relationship with the kingdoms of nature only when it is
tempered by love and wisdom. In earlier times this truth was
presented in pictorial form and the soul was helped to under-

stand what we to-day express differently. Men were told
that the King's son rang the bell once and the Eagle-King
appeared; twice and the Fox-King appeared; three times and
the Fish-King appeared. It was they who brought back the
horse. In other words: the tumults which rage in the human
soul must be recognised; when they are recognised the soul
can be freed from lower influences and brought into order.

In the modern age we say that man must learn how his
passions, his anger and so on, are connected with his development from one seven-year period to another. In other words,
we must learn to understand the threefold sheaths of the
human being. In earlier times a wonderful picture was
placed before men: the King's son was given a mantle, a
sheath, every time he rang the little bell—that is to say, when
he had subjugated one of the kingdoms of nature. To-day we
speak of studying the nature of the physical body; in earlier
days a picture was used—of the Dragon-mother giving the
King's son a cloak or mantle of copper. We study the nature
of the etheric body; in earlier times it was said that the
Dragon-mother gave the King's son a silver cloak on the
second day. We speak of the astral body with its surging
passions; in earlier times it was said that on the third day the
Dragon-mother gave the King's son a cloak of gold. What
we learn to-day about the threefold nature of man in the
form of concepts was conveyed through the picture of the
copper, silver and golden cloaks. Instead of the pictures of
the copper, silver and golden cloaks we speak to-day in terms
which convey an understanding of how the solid physical
body is related to the other sheaths of the human being as
copper ore is related to silver and gold.

We speak to-day of seven classes of Luciferic beings whose
development was retarded during the Moon-evolution and
who set about bringing their influence to bear upon man's
astral body. The minstrels said: When the King's son came
to the mountain where he was to be united with the Flower-
Queen's daughter, he encountered seven dragons who would
have devoured him if he had not accomplished his task. We

know that if our evolution does not proceed in the right way it will be corrupted by the forces of the sevenfold Luciferic beings. We say nowadays that by achieving spiritual development we find our higher Self. The minstrels said: The King's son was united with the Flower-Queen. And we say: A certain rhythm must be established in the human soul. You will remember that a few weeks ago I said that when an idea has arisen in the soul we must allow time for the idea to mature, and it will then be possible to detect a certain rhythm in the process. After seven days the idea has penetrated into the depths of the soul; after fourteen days the maturing idea can lay hold of the outer astral substance and allow itself to be baptised by the World-Spirit. After twenty-one days the idea has become still more mature. And only after four times seven days is it ready to be offered to the world as a gift of our own personality. This is the manifestation of an inner rhythm of the soul. A man's creative faculty can work effectively only if he does not try immediately to force upon the world something that occurs to him but is aware that the ordered rhythm of the external world repeats itself in his soul, that he must live in such a way that the Macrocosm is reflected in the Microcosm of his own being. The minstrels said: Man must bring the forces of his soul into harmony, must seek the Flower-Queen's daughter and enter into a union with her during which he spends half of the year with his bride and for the other half leaves her to be with her mother who lives in the depths. This means that he establishes a rhythm within himself and the rhythm of his life takes its course in harmony with the rhythm of the Macrocosm.

These pictures—and hundreds like them could be mentioned—stimulated the soul through the thought-forms they created; and the result is that souls living to-day have become sufficiently mature to listen to the different kind of presentation given by Spiritual Science. But before this could happen man had perforce to experience a sense of deprivation and intense longing. The spiritual longings of the soul had first to be engulfed in the physical world. This did in fact happen in the first half of the nineteenth century; and then, in the second half of the century, came the materialistic culture with its devastating effect upon spiritual life. But the longing grew all the stronger and the ideal of the spiritual-scientific Movement became all the more significant. In the first half of the century there were only few who in a kind of silent martyrdom felt that ideas once conveyed in the form of pictures in narratives still survived but only in a state of decline.

In the soul of a man born in the year 1803, echoes of the old wisdom of past times were still reverberating. Something closely akin to theosophical ideas was a living reality in him. His soul was completely engrossed in what we to-day call the spiritual-scientific solution of the riddle of world-existence. His name was *Julius Mosen*. His soul was able to survive only because for most of his life he was bedridden. Soul and body could not adjust themselves to each other because owing to the way in which Mosen had grasped these ideas without being able to penetrate them spiritually, his etheric body had been drawn out of his physical body which was paralysed as a result. His soul had nevertheless risen to spiritual heights. In 1831 he wrote a remarkable book, *Ritter Wahn*. He had learnt of a wonderful legend still surviving in Italy, an old Italian folk-legend. As he studied it he became convinced that it enshrined something of the spirit of the universe, that those who created its imagery were filled with the living spirituality of the World Order. The result was that in 1831 he wrote a truly wonderful work—which, needless to say, has been forgotten, in common with so much that is the product of spiritual greatness.

Ritter Wahn sets out to conquer death and on his way he comes across three old men—Ird, Time and Space. Julius Mosen hit on the German word *Ird* to translate the Italian *il mondo*, because he knew that there was something particularly significant in it. Ird, Time and Space are the names of the three old men who, however, can be of no use to Ritter

Wahn because they are themselves subject to death. Ird denotes everything that is subject to the laws of the physical body, and so to death; Time, the etheric body, is by its very nature transitory; and the third, the lower astral body, which gives us the perception of Space, is also subject to death. Our individuality passes from incarnation to incarnation; but according to the Italian folk-legend, Ird, Time and Space represent our threefold sheath.

Who is 'Ritter Wahn?' Each of us, passing from incarnation to incarnation, looks out upon the world and faces maya, the great Illusion; each of us, in that we live a life in the spirit, goes forth to conquer death. On this quest we meet the three old men who are our three sheaths. They are indeed very old! The physical body has existed since the evolutionary period of Old Saturn, the etheric body since the period of Old Sun, and the astral body since the period of Old Moon. The Ego, the 'I', has been embodied in men in the course of the *Earth* period itself. Julius Mosen depicts Ritter Wahn seeking to overcome death. He uses the Platonic image of a rider on horseback—an image that was known all over Middle Europe and still farther afield. Ritter Wahn rides out in an attempt to conquer the heavens with materialistic thinking—like those who cling to the sense-world and are imprisoned in illusion and maya. But when through death they enter the spiritual world, what happens is faithfully described by Julius Mosen. Such human beings have not lived out their lives to the full and long to come down again to the Earth in order that their souls may continue to evolve. So Ritter Wahn returns to the Earth. He sees the beautiful Morgana, the soul, which is destined to be stimulated by whatever is earthly and—like the Flower-Queen's daughter —represents the union with what man can acquire only through schooling on Earth. He falls a victim to death through being again united with the Earth and the beautiful Morgana. This means that he passes through death in order that he may raise his own soul, represented by Morgana, to higher and higher stages during each succeeding incarnation.

It is from pictures like these which carry the stamp of their thousands of years' life that ideas stream into artists of the calibre of Julius Mosen. In his case they were given expression by a soul too great to live healthily in a physical body during the approaching age of materialism and Julius Mosen had consequently to endure the silent martyrdom imposed on him by his passionate soul.—Such was the impulse at work in a man living in the first half of the nineteenth century. It will become active again but in such a way as to kindle human powers and forces; and it will enable us to have some understanding of what is meant by the spirit of Rosicrucianism—the spirit that must make its way into the souls of men.

We can now surmise that what we ourselves are cultivating has always existed. Were we to imagine that anything in the world can prosper without this spirit working in men we should be succumbing to the delusions suffered by Ritter Wahn.

Whence came the minstrels of the seventh, eighth or even thirteenth centuries, wandering as they did through the world to create thought-forms that would enable souls in our own day to have a different kind of understanding? Where had these minstrels learnt how to bring such pictures to men? They had learnt from the centres we think of to-day as the Rosicrucian schools. They were pupils of Rosi-crucians. Their teachers said to them: You cannot now go forth into the world and clothe your message in concepts and ideas, as will have to be done later on; you must speak of the King's son, of the Flower-Queen and of the three cloaks, in order that from these pictures thought-forms may come into being and live in the souls of men. And when these souls return to Earth they will understand what is needed for their further progress.—Messengers are continually sent out from the centres of spiritual life in order that in every age what lies in the depths of the spirit may be made accessible to men.

It is a superficial view to believe that such tales can be

invented by human fancy. The old tales which give expression to the spiritual secrets of the world came into being because those who composed them gave ear to others who were able to impart the spiritual secrets. Consequently we can say with truth that the spirit of all humanity, of the Microcosm and the Macrocosm, lives in them.

The minstrels were sent out to tell their stories from the same centres whence we to-day draw the knowledge on which the culture needed by humanity is based. Thus it is that the spirit in which mankind is rooted moves on from epoch to epoch. The Beings who in pre-Christian times imparted instruction to individuals in the temples, teaching them what they had themselves brought over from former planetary evolutions—these Beings placed themselves under the leadership of Christ, the unique Individuality who became the great Teacher and Guide of mankind. Stories which have come down through the centuries and have inspired in the whole of Western culture thought-forms expressing in pictures the same teaching about Christ as we give to-day, make it quite clear that in the period after the Mystery of Golgotha the spiritual leadership of mankind, working through its centres of learning, was vested in Christ. All spiritual leadership is connected with Him. If we can make ourselves conscious of this fact we shall be turning our gaze to the light we need in order to understand the longings of human souls incarnated in the nineteenth century.

If we think deeply about souls who reveal the longings of earlier times, we shall recognise with a sense of profound responsibility that they waited for us to bring their longings to fulfilment. Julius Mosen, the author of *Ritter Wahn* and *Ahasver*, and others like him, were the last prophets of the West because the teachings once given by messengers from the holy temples in the form of pictures to prepare souls for later ages, were living realities to them. And their yearning is indicated in words written by Rothe of Heidelberg in 1847: '. . . if theosophy ever becomes scientific in the real sense and produces obvious and definite results, these will gradually become the general conviction, be acknowledged as valid truths and be universally accepted by those who cannot find their way along the only possible path by which they could be discovered . . .' At that time a man who had these yearnings—thinking not only of himself but also of his contemporaries—could only say with resignation that all this lay in the womb of the future which he had no wish to anticipate. In 1847, men who were cognisant of the secrets of the Rosicrucian temples had not yet spoken in a way that could be generally understood. But what lies in the womb of the future can become living power if there are enough souls who realise that knowledge is a duty—a duty because we must not give back undeveloped souls to the World-Spirit. Were we to do that we should have deprived the World-Spirit of forces implanted in us. If there are souls who recognise their duty to the World-Spirit and endeavour to understand the riddles of the world, the hopes cherished by the best men of earlier times will be fulfilled. They looked to us, who were to be born after them, and longed that theosophy should become scientifically acceptable and lay hold of the hearts of men. But these hearts must exist! And that depends upon people who have identified themselves with our spiritual-scientific Movement being convinced of the need for spiritual illumination of the riddles of existence. It depends upon every single soul among us whether the longings of which I have spoken prove to have been empty dreams on the part of those who had hoped for the best in us or to have been dreams now brought to fulfilment.

When we see the barrenness of science, art and every domain of social life we must tell ourselves that we need not succumb to it but that there is a way out. For again an age has dawned when voices from the holy temples are speaking —not in pictures and stories but proclaiming truths which many people still regard as theories but which can and must become sources of life and nourishment to the soul. Each individual can resolve with the highest powers of his soul to receive this source of life.

This is what we must impress upon our souls as the epitome of the meaning and spirit of the guidance of mankind. If we allow this thought to be active in our souls it will be an impulse in us for many months. We shall find that it can grow into an impressive structure—quite independently of the words used to express it. My words may well be imperfect but it is the reality in the thought that matters, not the form in which it is expressed. This reality can live in every single soul. The totality of truth is present in every soul as a seed and can be brought to blossom if the soul devotes itself to the development of that seed.

KYRIOS, THE LORD OF THE SOUL

In several lecture-courses* given over the years in the different Groups and attended by many of the friends here to-day, we have endeavoured to study the Gospels of St. John, St. Luke and St. Matthew and the great event in Palestine, the Mystery of Golgotha, from three different points of view.

One result of these studies should have been to establish in our souls a growing realisation of the greatness of this unique event. We have understood that the reason why there are four Gospels is that their authors, writing as inspired occultists, each wished to describe the great event from a special angle, just as a photograph of an object is taken from a particular side. By combining the pictures, each taken from a different angle, an idea of the reality can be obtained. Each of the Evangelists makes it possible for us to study one aspect in particular of the great event in Palestine.

The Gospel of St. John gives us insight into the great events in Palestine by opening out a vista of the highest human goals and at the same time of the sublime realities of the spiritual worlds.

The Gospel of St. Luke unveils the mysteries connected with the personality of Jesus of Nazareth, with the Solomon Jesus and the Nathan Jesus, until the moment when the Christ descends into him.

The Gospel of St. Matthew, as those of you who heard the lectures will know and others will be able to read, shows how the bodily nature in which the Christ was to incarnate for three years was prepared by mysterious processes connected with the racial stock of the ancient Hebrew people.

* See list of publications on page 221.

In a certain respect the Gospel of St. Mark can lead us to supreme heights in our study of Christianity and give us insight into many matters communicated by the other Gospels but in a less dramatic way. And so this evening I will take the opportunity of saying something in reference to the Gospel of St. Mark.

We must realise how necessary it is to study many subjects with which superficial modern thought has no inclination to concern itself. If we are to understand the Gospel of St. Mark in its depths we must acquaint ourselves to some extent with the very different character of the language in which men expressed themselves at the time when Christ Jesus was on the Earth. Let me try to convey to you what I mean by using contrasts as it were of light and shadow.

We make use of language to express what we want to say and to reveal what lives in our souls. It is in the way in which language is used as a means of expressing the inner life of soul that the several epochs in the evolution of humanity differ radically from one another. If we go back to the ancient Hebrew epoch and to the wonderful modes of expression used in the temple-language, we find that there was a quite different way of clothing the secrets of the soul in words—a way undreamed of nowadays. In the old Hebrew language only the consonants were written, the vowels being inserted afterwards; and when a word was uttered the echoes of a whole world reverberated in it—not, as is the case to-day, some more or less abstract concept. The reason why the vowels were not written was that they were an indication of the speaker's inmost being, whereas the consonants were intended to depict external objects or conditions. For example, whenever an ancient Hebrew wrote the letter B—or what corresponded to our present B—it always evoked in him a sense of warmth and a picture of some outer condition, in this case something in which one could be enclosed, as in a shelter or a house. The sound B could not be uttered without this feeling as an accompaniment. Again, the sound A (ah) could not be uttered without conveying the impression or image of something inwardly powerful, of a radiating force. The content of the soul thus projected into words streamed out into space and into other souls. Language was therefore much more alive, much more related to the secrets of existence than is the case nowadays.

This is one side—the light side I wanted to convey. But there is also the other side—the shadow side—constituted by the fact that in the use of our language we have to a great extent become utterly shallow. Our language expresses only abstractions, generalisations. People no longer have any feeling about this but it could not be otherwise in times when language is used, even for literary purposes, before writers have any spiritual content to convey, when enormous masses of printed matter circulate everywhere, when everyone feels that he must write something and nothing is considered unsuitable as subject-matter. When our Society was founded I discovered that certain authors were attaching themselves to it simply out of curiosity, in the hope of finding material for their novels. Why, they thought, should they not find characters among the Members who could be portrayed in their stories? So it behoves us to realise that our language nowadays has become abstract, commonplace and vacuous and there is neither a sense of its holiness nor, as was once the case, a feeling of responsibility towards its use. That is why it is so extraordinarily difficult to put into modern words the great facts proclaimed by the Gospels. People cannot understand that our modern language is empty when compared, for example, with the fulness of meaning implicit in a word of the ancient Greek language. When we read the Bible to-day we are reading something that in comparison with the original wording has been sifted not once but two or three times, and it is not the best but the worst that has remained. It does, of course, seem natural to quote from modern versions of the Bible, but we go astray most disastrously of all when we quote the Gospel of St. Mark in its modern rendering.

You know that at the very beginning of the Gospel of St.

Mark, in Weizsäcker's supposedly excellent translation—although as might be guessed from the high reputation it enjoys to-day, it is anything but excellent!—these words are found:

> "As it is written in the prophet Isaiah: Behold I send my messenger before you who shall prepare the way before you. Listen how the voice is heard in the wilderness: Prepare the way of the Lord, make his paths straight."*

When we read a passage like this it would be self-deception to pretend that we understand it; if we are honest we shall admit that it is utterly incomprehensible to us. The passage is either of no significance or it says something we cannot understand. The first thing to do, then, is to assemble concepts enabling us to grasp the meaning of this saying of Isaiah. Isaiah was referring to the event which was to be of supreme significance for the evolution of humanity. What has already been said gives some indication of what Isaiah was foretelling in these words.

In ancient days man was endowed with a kind of clairvoyance and through the forces of his soul was able to rise into the divine-spiritual world. When this happened he was not using his Ego, his 'I', at the stage of development it had then reached; he was using his astral body which contained the powers of seership, whereas the forces rooted in the Ego were only gradually being awakened by perception of the physical world. The 'I' uses physical instruments, but in earlier times, if a man were seeking revelation, he used his astral body, seeing and perceiving through it. The process of evolution itself consisted in the transition from use of the astral body to use of the 'I'. The Christ Impulse was to be the most powerful factor in the development of the 'I'. If the

* The words in the English Authorised Version are:

'As it is written in the Prophets, Behold, I send my messenger before thy face, which shall prepare thy way before thee. The voice of one crying in the wilderness, Prepare ye the way of the Lord, make his paths straight.'

words of St. Paul: 'Not I but Christ in me' are fulfilled in the 'I', then the 'I' is able to grow into the spiritual world through its own forces, whereas formerly this was possible only for the astral body.

This, then, is how evolution proceeded: Man once used his astral body as an organ of perception, but the astral body became less and less able to serve that purpose. When the time of Christ's coming was drawing near, it was losing its power to see into the spiritual world. Man could no longer be united with that world through his astral body and the 'I' was not yet strong enough to reveal it. That was the state of things when the time of Christ's coming was approaching.

In the course of human evolution the important steps which are eventually to take place have always to be prepared in advance. This was so in the case of the Christ Impulse too; but there was necessarily a period of transition. There could be no sudden change from the time when man felt his astral body becoming unreceptive to the spiritual world, becoming barren and desolate, to a time when the 'I' was kindled into activity through the Christ Impulse. What happened was that as the result of a certain influence from the spiritual world a few human beings were able to experience in the astral body something of what was later to be seen and known by the 'I'. Egohood was prepared for, anticipated as it were in the astral body. It was through the 'I' and its development that man became Earth-Man in the real sense. The astral body properly belonged to the evolutionary period of the Old Moon, when the *Angels* were at the human stage. Man is at the human stage on the Earth. On the Old Moon it was appropriate for man to use his astral body. Everything else was merely preparation for the development of the 'I'. The earliest stages of Earth-evolution proper were a recapitulation of the Old Moon-evolution, for man could never become fully man in the astral body; on the Old Moon it was only the Angels who could reach the human stage in the astral body. And just as the Christ lived in earthly man in order to inspire his 'I', so there were Angels who, having reached the human stage on the Old Moon, prophetically inspired man's astral body as a preparation for Egohood. A time was to come in human evolution on the Earth when man would be ready for the development of the 'I'. On the Old Moon the Angels had developed to the highest stage, but as we have heard, only in the astral body. Now, in order that man might be prepared for Egohood, it was necessary that in exceptional conditions, and through grace, certain individuals should be inspired to work on the Earth as Angels; although they were men, the reality was that Angels were working in and through them.

This is a concept of great importance, without which there can be no understanding of human evolution in line with that of occultism. It is easy enough to say simply that everything is maya, but that is a mere abstraction. We must be able to say: Yes, a man is standing in front of me, but he is maya—indeed who knows if he is really a man? Perhaps what seems to be a human figure is only the outer sheath; perhaps some quite other being is using this sheath in order to accomplish a task that is beyond man's capacity.—I have given an indication of this in *The Portal of Initiation*.

Such an event in the history of humanity actually took place when the Individuality who had lived in Elijah was reborn as John the Baptist. An Angel entered into the soul of John the Baptist in that incarnation, using his bodily nature and also his soul to accomplish what no human being could have accomplished. In John the Baptist there lived an Angel whose mission was to herald in advance the Egohood that was to be present in its fulness in Jesus of Nazareth. It is of the greatest importance to realise that John the Baptist was maya and that an Angel, a Messenger, was living in him. This is indeed what the Greek says: Lo, I send my Messenger. The Messenger is an Angel. But nobody pays attention to what is actually said here. A deep mystery, enacted in the Baptist and foretold by Isaiah, is indicated. Isaiah foretold that the future John the Baptist would be maya—in reality he was to be the vehicle for the Angel, the Messenger who was to proclaim what man will become if he takes the Christ Impulse into himself. Angels announce in advance what man will later become. The passage in question might therefore be translated: Lo, the bestower of Egohood sends his Messenger (Angel) before you to whom Egohood is to be given.

Let us now see if we can discover the meaning of the third sentence. We must first try to picture the conditions prevailing in man's inner life when the astral body had gradually lost the power to send out its forces like feelers and to see clairvoyantly into the divine-spiritual world. Formerly, when the astral body was activated, man was able to look into that world, but this faculty was disappearing and darkness spreading within him. He had once been able to expand his astral body over all the beings of the spiritual world, but now he was inwardly desolate, inwardly isolated— the Greek word is ἔρημος. At that time the human soul lived in isolation, in desolation. This is what the Greek text tells us: Lo, a voice seems to speak in the desolation of the soul— call it 'wilderness' of the soul if you like—when the astral body can no longer expand into the divine-spiritual world. Hear the cry in the wilderness, in the desolation of the soul!

What is it that is being proclaimed in advance? First of all we must be clear about the meaning of the word *Kyrios*, when it was used in Hebrew but also still in Greek in reference to manifestations of the soul and spirit. To translate it simply as 'the Lord', with the usual connotation, is sheer nonsense. In ancient times everyone using the word *Kyrios* knew perfectly well that its meaning was connected with the development of man's soul-life and its mysteries. In the astral body, as we know, are the forces of thinking, feeling and willing; the soul thinks, feels and wills. These are the three forces working in the soul but they are actually its servants. In earlier times man was under their domination and he obeyed them, but as his evolution progressed these forces were to become the servants of the Kyrios, the Ruler, the Lord—in short, of the 'I'. Used in relation to the soul, the word Kyrios actually meant the 'I'. At this stage it would no longer be true to say: 'The Divine-Spiritual thinks, feels and wills in me', but rather: 'I think, I feel, I will.' The passage should be rendered more or less as follows.—Prepare yourselves, you human souls, to move along those paths that will awaken the Kyrios, the powerful 'I' within you; listen to the cry in the solitude of the soul. Make ready the path (or way) of the 'I', the Lord of the soul. Open the way for his forces so that he may no longer be the slave but the Ruler of thinking, feeling and willing. Lo, the power that is the 'I' sends his Angel before you, the Angel who is to give you the possibility of understanding the cry in the solitude of the astral soul. Prepare the paths of the 'I', open the way for the forces of the 'I'.—Such is the meaning of these significant words of the prophet Isaiah; they point to the greatest of all events in the evolution of humanity. You will now understand the sense in which he speaks about the future John the Baptist, indicating how man's soul in its solitude longs for the coming of its Lord and Ruler, the 'I'. Such is the real meaning of this passage and in this sense it is to be understood.

Why was John the Baptist able to be the bearer of the Angel? It was because he had received a particular form of Initiation. Initiations are not all identical in character and individuals who have a definite mission to fulfil must undergo a special form of Initiation. Now the writing of the stars in the heavens is so ordered as to reveal the nature and facts of happenings in the spiritual world. Thus a man may receive the Sun-Initiation, which means that he is initiated into the mysteries of the spiritual world of Ahura Mazdao—the spiritual world of which the Sun is the outer expression. But there are twelve forms of the Sun-Initiation, each of which differs from the other eleven. A man will receive a particular form of Initiation according to the mission he is to fulfil for humanity. His Initiation, though still a Sun-Initiation, may be of such a kind that the forces stream in as they do when the Sun is standing, for instance, in the constellation of Cancer; and these forces will be very different in the case of an Initiation connected with the Sun

in Libra. These are the expressions used to indicate specialised Initiations. Individuals chosen for a mission as lofty as
that of John the Baptist must receive Initiation in the form
that can give the strength necessary for the fulfilment of
their mission. And so in order that he might become the
bearer of the Angel, John the Baptist received the Sun-
Initiation originating from the constellation of Aquarius. The
Sun in Aquarius is the symbol for the form of Initiation
received by John the Baptist in order that he might become
the bearer of the Angel. He received the Sun-forces which
flow when the Sun is standing in Aquarius—the Waterman.
The sign was the symbol indicating that John the Baptist had
received this particular Initiation. In actual fact the name
Aquarius, or Waterman, was given to the zodiacal sign
because those who had received that Initiation acquired the
faculty which enabled John the Baptist, for example, to
achieve what he did. When men were plunged under water,
their etheric bodies were momentarily loosened and in that
condition it was possible for them to perceive what action
was of the greatest importance at that particular time.
Baptism in the Jordan revealed to those who underwent it
the momentous significance of that period in history. It was
to this end that John had received the baptismal Initiation
and because this was connected with the rays of the Sun
streaming from its position in a particular constellation, the
constellation too was known symbolically as the Waterman.
The name of the constellation was derived from the human
faculty connected with it, and not vice versa.

Nowadays many learned ignoramuses try to explain
spiritual happenings of this character by bringing Heaven
down to Earth, saying that such things are simply indications
of the movement of the Sun through the Zodiac. These
learned gentlemen, who fundamentally know nothing,
explain events in humanity by reference to the heavens. In
the case of John the Baptist, actually the opposite was true:
the zodiacal sign was used to express something that had
occurred on Earth and was then transferred to the Heavens.

John the Baptist could therefore rightly say: 'I baptise you with water.' This was the same as saying to his intimate disciples, as he might well have done, that he had received the Aquarius Initiation. The movement of the Sun through the Zodiac as seen with physical eyes is in the direction from Leo to Virgo; the spiritual movement is from Aquarius to Pisces. Consequently John the Baptist was able to proclaim something that would work as the forces of the Sun in Pisces and not in Aquarius; also that the Being who was to come would give a higher kind of Baptism than he himself was able to give. The spiritual Sun progresses from Aquarius to Pisces and when this happens the Aquarius Baptism becomes a Baptism with *spiritual* water—Pisces, the Fishes. Hence the ancient symbol of fishes for the Being who was the bearer of the Christ. Just as John, through very special influences, had received the Aquarius Initiation, so all the mysteries enacted around and in Jesus of Nazareth belonged to a Pisces Initiation. The Sun had moved forward, spiritually, from one zodiacal constellation to another, indicating that Jesus of Nazareth had passed through a Pisces Initiation.

All this is hinted at in St. Mark's Gospel but such things have to be presented in pictures. Christ Jesus draws to Himself those who are seeking that of which Pisces is the symbol. Hence His first disciples are all of them fishermen. The indication of the Sun's progression into Pisces is clear when we read the words of John the Baptist: 'I have baptised you with water, but He will baptise you with the Holy Spirit.' And as Christ passes along the shore of the Sea of Galilee, that is to say, when the Sun has moved so far that its counterpart could be seen rising in Pisces, the fishermen known as Simon and Simon's brother, James and James's brother, are inspired to follow Him.

How can we understand all this? We shall not understand it unless we go more deeply into the linguistic expressions used in those times. Our modern way of expressing ourselves is slovenly and banal. Thus when a human being is standing in front of us, we say: Here is a man—similarly when there

are two or three. But what is there in front of us is only maya;
if we see a being with two legs and a human face the only
way of expressing what we see in our modern language is to
say: That is a man. But what does occultism take this 'man'
to be? In the form in which he stands before us he is nothing
but maya—approximately as real as a rainbow in the sky. A
rainbow is a reality only as long as the necessary conditions
of rain and sunshine are present; as soon as the relation
between sunshine and rain changes, the rainbow vanishes. It
is exactly the same in the case of a man. He is only a confluence of forces of the Macrocosm; we must look for forces
in the heavens, in the Macrocosm. For the occultist, what we
assume on Earth to be a man is simply nothingness. The
truth is that forces are streaming from above downwards and
from below upwards, and they intersect. And just as a
particular combination of rain and sun produces a rainbow,
so do forces streaming together from above and from below
out of the Macrocosm create a phenomenon, an illusory
image, which we take to be a man. But the man we see
before us is really nothing but maya. Where we think we see
a man there are intersecting cosmic forces. You must take
this quite seriously. The man as he stands before us is
merely a shadow of many forces. But the being who mani-
fests in the man may well be at a different place altogether
from the point where the man with his two legs is standing.

Now think of three human beings. One is a peasant in
ancient Persia, working his plough in the Persian countryside. He looks like a man, but in reality he is a soul whose
forces are sustained by some world from above or from
below, and if we are to have real knowledge of him we must
ascend to the realm of these forces. The second man is
possibly some kind of official in ancient Persia. He too is
formed from another world through intersecting forces and
again, if we are to know him in the real sense, we must
ascend to the realm of those forces. Finally, think of a third
Persian, or one of whom we should have to say even more
emphatically: he is a veritable illusion, a phantom. To

discover the truth about him we should have to ascend to the
Sun to find the forces sustaining this phantom figure. There
above, among the mysteries of the Sun, we should find what
we might call the Golden Star—Zarathustra. Rays are sent
down and on the Earth there lives the being we call Zarathustra, though his essential being is not there at all.

The important thing is to realise that in ancient times men
were well aware of the significance of names. Names were not
given as they are to-day but according to what was really
living in a human being, apart altogether from the outer
appearance. An old man at the time of Christ would have
understood very well what was meant if someone had
pointed to John the Baptist, saying: There is the Angel of
God! The outer appearance would have been disregarded as
a secondary consideration and attention paid only to the
inner reality.—And now suppose the same mode of expression had been used in connection with Christ Jesus.
What would have been said of Him in times when such
things were understood? Nobody would have so much as
dreamed of giving the appellation Christ Jesus to the body
of flesh moving about the land; the body was regarded
merely as the sign that what was streaming down spiritually
from the Sun had gathered together at this particular point.
And when this body—the body of Jesus—moved from one
place to another it was simply that the Sun-force was being
made visible. This Sun-force was able of itself to move from
place to place, independently of a physical body. Occasionally, Christ Jesus was said to be 'in the house', that is to say,
in the flesh; but the Being in the flesh also moved about
without a body. In the Gospel of St. John, above all, the
Evangelist often writes exactly as if the Sun-force were
present in a body of flesh when in reality the Christ is
moving from place to place purely in the spirit.

That is why it is so important for the deeds of Christ Jesus
always to be brought into relationship with the physical Sun
—which is the outward expression for the spiritual world
when gathered together at the point where the physical body

is present. For example, when Christ Jesus performs an act of healing, it is the Sun-force that heals, but the Sun must be in the right position in the heavens. Thus: 'At even, when the sun did set they brought unto Him all that were diseased. . . .' and so on. It was important to indicate that this healing force can flow down only when the physical Sun has set and is working in a purely spiritual way. Again when Christ Jesus needs special power in order to do His works, He must draw it from the spiritual Sun, not from the physically visible Sun. 'And in the morning, rising up a great while before day, He went out . . .' The path of the Sun and the power of the Sun are expressly indicated, furthermore that it is the Sun-force that is working, that Jesus is simply the external sign and that this path taken by the Sun-force could also become visible to the naked eye. Wherever St. Mark's Gospel speaks of the Christ, what is meant is the Sun-force which, in that epoch of Earth-evolution, worked with special strength upon the land called Palestine. Moreover the Sun-force, gathered into a focus, was moving from place to place, and the body of Jesus was the outward sign making the movement of the Sun-force visible to physical sight. The paths of Jesus in Palestine were the paths of the Sun-force that had come down to the Earth. If you trace the paths of Jesus to form a kind of chart you will have before you the indication of a cosmic happening—the Sun-force had penetrated into the land of Palestine. It is a macrocosmic process—that is the essential point. This is made especially evident by the writer of St. Mark's Gospel, who was well aware that a body which was the bearer of a principle such as the Christ-Principle must be entirely subservient to it. The Gospel therefore directs attention to the world so gloriously proclaimed by Zarathustra—the world which lies behind the material world and influences the life of man. Through Christ Jesus it was again made clear how the forces of this spiritual world work into the Earth. Hence in the body—the body of the Nathan Jesus as we have heard*—which was influenced in a

* See Lecture-Course on the *Gospel of St. Luke*, lectures IV–VII.

particular way by the Zarathustra-Individuality, it was inevitable that a kind of repetition should take place of happenings connected with Zarathustra.

We know some of the beautiful legends about Zarathustra. Almost immediately after his birth occurred the first miracle, that known as the 'Zarathustra smile'. The second miracle was when Duransurun, the King ruling the district where Zarathustra was born, determined to murder the child about whom retrograde Magi had made certain statements. But when the King was on the point of stabbing the child his arm was paralysed. Finding that he could not use his dagger to do away with the child, he ordered him to be taken out into the wilderness and left among the wild beasts. This is the expression used to indicate that already in earliest childhood Zarathustra was destined to see what everyone is bound to see if his gaze has not been cleansed of impurities. Instead of the majestic Group-Souls and the higher spiritual Beings, he sees the emanations of his untamed fantasies. This is what is meant when we are told that Zarathustra was left in the wilderness among the wild beasts, but remained unharmed. This was the third miracle; the fourth was again connected with wild beasts. And always it was the good spirits of Ahura Mazdao who ministered to him.

These miracles are to some extent repeated in St. Mark's Gospel. 'And immediately the Spirit driveth him into the wilderness' (the word really means solitude). 'And he was there in the wilderness forty days, tempted of Satan; and was with the wild beasts; and the angels ministered unto him.'

It is made clear to us here that the body was being prepared to become a focus of macrocosmic processes. What had happened to Zarathustra had to be repeated in the encounter with the wild beasts. The body became the bearer of macrocosmic processes.

In its very first lines the Gospel of St. Mark presents us with a vista of majestic grandeur and my aim in this lecture has been to show you how this Gospel acquires new life and power if only the words are understood in their right sense—

not in that of our commonplace modern speech but in the sense of ancient language, when whole worlds lay behind each word. Our modern language needs to be recast in many ways before it is possible to discover what the words of ancient languages contained. When we say that man lives on the Earth and develops his 'I', or that he was present on the Old Moon when it was the Angels who reached their human stage—all this must be borne in mind when we read: Behold, I send my Angel before men. These words cannot be understood without the preliminary knowledge communicated by Spiritual Science.

If people were really honest to-day they would admit that the words at the beginning of St. Mark's Gospel are unintelligible to them. But instead they adopt an arrogant attitude and maintain that Spiritual Science is so much fantasy and puts all kinds of complications into what would otherwise be quite simple. But the fact of the matter is that people to-day have no real knowledge; they no longer recognise the principle adopted, for instance, in ancient Persia, when the sacred records were re-written from epoch to epoch in order to be clothed in a new form suited to every period. In this way the divine Word was recast in the form of the Zend Avesta, then again recast, and what we have to-day is its latest form. The Persian scriptures were, in fact, re-written seven times. One of the tasks of Anthroposophy is to teach men how necessary it is that records in which sacred mysteries are clothed in words should be re-written from epoch to epoch. For if we want to preserve the sublime language of the ancient writings we should not attempt in our re-writing to adhere pedantically to the old words; we should rather try to translate them into words that are immediately intelligible in the present age. An attempt to do this was made in the summer in the lecture-course on *Genesis: The Bible Story of Creation,* and you will have realised then how many of the words must be re-cast. The lecture to-day may have given you some idea of how the same principle applies to the Gospel of St. Mark.

MYSTERY TEACHINGS IN ST. MARK'S GOSPEL

In the course of the years we have spoken about the deeper meanings of the Gospels of St. Matthew, St. Luke and St. John, and here in Hanover, too, about the mysteries of Christianity. You will have realised that each of the Gospels provides a special means of penetrating to the core of the Christian message. It is almost truer to say of the Gospel of St. Mark than of the others that if it is to help us to gain some understanding of Christianity, we must make a certain basic assumption.

In studying this Gospel it is essential to be aware of how language was used as a means of expression in past ages of evolution. The ancient Hebrew language opens up a wide horizon in this respect. Those of you who were present at the lecture-course in Munich on *Genesis: The Bible Story of Creation*, must have realised how necessary it was to give an adequate translation of particular words before the six or seven days' work of creation could be understood, and how essential it is to re-create these ancient records in order to bring to light the inner, spiritual truths they indicate. In the Hebrew language the vowels and consonants were used very differently from anything that is customary to-day. What a man saw round about him was indicated in that ancient language by the consonants; the vowels expressed inner experiences of the soul and were indicated by dots only. In those early times, and even in the Greek language, a word in itself was an indication of a supersensible reality. Everyone knew that a spoken word containing certain sounds or syllables would arouse in the soul a whole series of mental pictures. A very great deal could be conveyed in a few words because all these factors were operating. We must always bear this in mind when we are studying the Gospel of St. Mark. We must not restrict ourselves to the actual words, because the words by themselves cannot lead us into the secrets and mysteries of that Gospel.

Let me give you one or two illustrations. In earlier times, language was a means for the expression of realities of soul and spirit. In our day it is a means for the expression of abstract thinking and this is very far removed from the living, pictorial thinking which alone can point the way into spiritual worlds. If we want to recover that kind of living thinking we must alter the forms of expression in our language accordingly. Language has become pedantic, useful only as an expression of abstract thinking; it has entirely lost the living quality which is able to lead into higher regions through the words of language and to unite the soul with the mysteries of the Universe. In the Rosi-crucian Mystery Play, *The Portal of Initiation*, beginnings have been made to infuse real life into language. It is often a matter of subtle nuances. Our language is crude, lacks suppleness, and it is only with a struggle that it can be made to express the delicate aspects of spiritual life. That is why I tried to manipulate language in such a way as to point to secrets of existence. In the Mystery Play I made an attempt to use other means to express a great deal that words cannot express. In the Play a man is striving to take the first steps towards Initiation, to hear spiritual tones resounding in his soul. The Play describes the many deep experiences under-gone by Johannes in the course of his development. His progress is such that through the bitterest but at the same time the most powerful inner experiences, he reaches the realm of Devachan in the spiritual world where he is to be introduced to the life and activity of the elemental beings there. Any attempt to express this in ordinary words could only result in abstractions. And so I tried to present living people, expressing in their own nature the mysteries of how light and darkness interweave. In this way I tried to make audible in actual sounds things which, expressed in the words of modern language, would have seemed unreal. One must listen intently to the sound of the words and feel how the right sound occurs at the right place, sensing where a sound is appropriate and where it is not. This is a kind of spiritual alchemy. And by such means it is possible to indicate the inter-weaving life and activity of the spiritual forces in the Universe.

In the Mystery Play, Johannes is welcomed in Devachan by Maria and her companions, Philia, Astrid and Luna. Philia is the poetic representation of the sentient soul, hence the sound I(ee) occurs twice and A once in her name. Luna is the expression of the consciousness-soul, hence U and A occur once in her name. Astrid, the expression of the intel-lectual or mind-soul has in her name first the sound A then I(ee). In this way a great deal can be expressed more truly than in words. If a feeling for such things could be aroused there is a great deal which I might be able to omit. You must learn to feel the significance of the U with its dull, deep ring, the lightness of the I(ee) and the delicate significance of the AI or EI, with the sense of wonder it awakens in the soul. This brings a kind of understanding different from any-thing to be gained through ordinary words. The sounds of language make it a most wonderful instrument, infinitely wiser than human beings, and it would be well for us to pay heed to its wisdom. Far from that, however, men are doing what they can to destroy it. If we want to have any under-standing at all of earlier times with their peculiar forms of expression, we must penetrate into what was then living in the souls of men.

When we read the lines at the very beginning of St. Mark's Gospel we can feel how necessary it is to think in this way about language and its secrets. In Luther's translation, which in most respects is still the best—Weizsäcker's is far inferior—the passage from Isaiah reads: 'Behold I send my Angel before thee who shall prepare thy way before thee. It is the voice of the preacher in the wilderness: "Prepare the way of the Lord, make straight his path".'

You would think that anyone who is honest with himself

would have to admit that he can make nothing of this passage. To understand what it really means Spiritual Science must enable us to recognise what, according to Isaiah who was initiated in these mysteries, was to come to pass through the events of Palestine and the Mystery of Golgotha. In our day nobody is willing to admit that there are men who really can tell us something important about the most significant impulses in world-evolution. Consequently we have grotesque explanations of the Apocalypse and assertions that the writer had himself already experienced the happenings described. People talk about objective research but always start with the assumption that what they do not know cannot be known. In the words just quoted, Isaiah is giving voice to something he knew through Initiation, namely that an impulse of supreme importance is to be given to the evolution of humanity. Why did he, and all other Initiates, regard this event to which he was pointing as being of such significance? His picture of the evolution of humanity was true and he knew that in earlier times men possessed a natural clairvoyance, moreover that through the astral body they were able to see into the spiritual worlds. The astral body gradually lost the power of vision and became inwardly dark but man's progress lay in this very loss of astral clairvoyance. It was now to be made possible for the 'I' to function. Out of his Initiation-knowledge Isaiah might also have said: In those days men will speak only of their Ego and as long as that Ego is not filled with Christ it will be restricted to perception of the physical plane furnished by the senses and intellect. Men will be forsaken by the world of the spirit. But then Christ will come, bringing consolation, and human souls will be permeated more and more with the Christ Impulse so that they can again look upwards into the spiritual world. Before this is possible, however, they will experience the darkening of the astral body.

The very first beginnings of man's physical body came into being on Old Saturn, of his etheric body on Old Sun, of his astral body on Old Moon; and the Ego evolves on the

Earth. Until the astral body lost its clairvoyant powers and became dark, the Ego had at first to work in the darkness. Before Earth-evolution began in the real sense a kind of recapitulation of the Moon-evolution took place. During that period man's astral body had developed to a stage where the activity of the whole Universe was mirrored within it. When the recapitulation of the Moon-evolution was completed the Ego began to enter into the process of evolution and Isaiah could say that Egohood would become more and more dominant on the Earth.

There were Beings who had reached the human stage on the Old Moon, others on Old Sun and Old Saturn. Man reached the human stage on the Earth. On the Old Moon the Angels reached the human stage and man has reached the human stage on the Earth. Consequently it devolved upon the Beings who were man's forerunners to make preparation for what man was to become on the Earth. The Angel-nature must penetrate into the astral body before the Ego can become active. Man's mission on Earth was prepared for by his forerunners—the Angels. Hence it is possible at certain times for an Angel to enter into a human personality. When this happens the Earth-man himself may well be maya, for a Being of higher rank is making use of his soul. The man is in truth the figure we see before us, yet he may be the sheath of some other Being. Thus it came about that the same Individuality who had once lived as Elijah and was reincarnated as John the Baptist became the vehicle of an Angel who spoke through him. In *The Portal of Initiation* a similar process takes place and another Being works in and through Maria:

> Within our circle there is formed a knot
> Of threads that Karma spins, world-fashioning.
> Thy sufferings, my friend, are links in chains
> Forged by the hand of destiny, whereby
> The deeds of Gods unite with human lives.
>
> (*The Portal of Initiation.* Scene 3)

A deed of the Gods mingles with human life and creates human destiny.

Thus in John the Baptist a deed of the Heavens was united with human destiny. A divine Being, an Angel, worked in and through him. What John achieved was possible only because, while the man John was maya, another Being lived within him, having the mission to proclaim in advance what man's destiny on Earth was to be. Consequently, if we are to translate the passage in a way that helps us to understand what is actually expressed, the rendering would have to be something like this.—'Take heed: the 'I' which is to appear in man's being sends in advance the Angel who prepares its way.' The Angel is the Being who lived in the personality of John the Baptist, and the lesson to be learnt from Spiritual Science is that Moon Initiates must make preparation for Initiations that belong essentially to the Earth.

We must now consider how man's nature had developed up to the time of the Mystery of Golgotha. Think of what men must have felt when they looked back to those past ages when the astral body could see clairvoyantly into the spiritual world, and then, as incarnation followed incarnation, realised that this astral body was growing steadily darker. In earlier times, when they wanted to observe something in the spiritual world their astral bodies became luminous and radiant. But this gradually ceased and darkness in the astral body intensified until there was within man a state of isolation, a wilderness, ἔρημος. Even in Greek the expression is to be found. Then a voice awakens in the human soul, like a cry of longing for the 'Lord', for the 'I', to enter into the soul. This was the feeling accompanying the word κύριος, translated so baldly as 'lord'. The soul was felt to consist of three forces: thinking, feeling and willing. Then a time came when the 'I', the *kyrios*, was to be received into the soul. This is what John the Baptist meant by the words: Prepare ye the way of the Lord, make his paths straight!

Thus the quotation from Isaiah at the beginning of St.

Mark's Gospel points to the wisdom-filled guidance of human evolution up to the time of the Mystery of Golgotha. This utterance of Isaiah also indicated what we now know about John the Baptist. I have described under what conditions he was able to become the vehicle of an Angel. A certain Initiation was necessary for this—the Initiation which enabled the man receiving it to reveal to other men that the time had now come for the 'I' to penetrate into the human soul.

This could be proclaimed only by one who had received the Initiation known since ancient times as the Aquarius Initiation in the terminology used in the Mysteries. The language of the heavens was used to express the great secrets of the spiritual world made known to men through Initiation. The language of the heavens alone is able to express what happens to the human soul when it is initiated into the great Mysteries. Such things cannot be described by human words. Men looked up to the stars, observed their relations to one another and said to themselves: if we can frame adequate expressions for what the stars reveal, that is the most fitting way to indicate the nature of the mysterious processes operating in a man during a particular Initiation.

No matter what name was used in the various civilisations, it was always the great Ahura Mazdao to whom men looked up: they looked up to that Divine Being and to his hierarchy in the Sun. Christ is the supreme Spirit of the Sun Beings. There are twelve different ways in which Initiation into the sacred Mysteries of the Sun can take place and to explain this in human words is hardly possible. But if we think of the Sun standing in one of the constellations and sending its rays through that constellation to the Earth, and if we consider how it is related to other stars, we have a kind of script which expresses the fact that a particular man is initiated into the Sun-Mysteries in a way that makes him an Aquarius Initiate.

Take, for instance, the seven holy Rishis. The symbol of their Initiation into the Sun-Mysteries is the picture of the

Sun in Taurus. When the Sun stands in the sign of Taurus the spectacle presented in the firmament reveals the mystery of the particular Initiation of the Rishis. This Initiation took effect through the seven personalities who were the seven holy Rishis. This is also expressed in the fact that the Pleiades, a cluster of seven stars, shine from the same region of the heavens. That is moreover the region where the whole solar system entered into the Universe to which we belong. So in order to specify the various forms of Initiation into the Sun-Mysteries we can use expressions indicating the Sun's position in a particular constellation.

John the Baptist had necessarily to receive an Aquarius Initiation, the expression indicating that the Sun was standing in the constellation of Aquarius. Try to understand it in this way: On the day or light side of the Zodiac lie Aries, Taurus, Gemini, Cancer, Leo, Virgo, then Libra. The constellations on the night or dark side of the Zodiac are Scorpio, Sagittarius, Capricorn, Aquarius and Pisces. Since the last two lie on the night side, the Sun's rays coming from them must not only traverse physical space but they must send the spiritual light of the Sun, which passes *through* the Earth, through spiritual space. Aquarius Initiates received this name because they were able to confer the water-baptism, that is to say, to enable men, while immersed in water, to be sustained by the power of the spiritual Sun.

It is the facts of the spiritual life here on Earth from which the names of the zodiacal constellations are derived, by transference to the heavens. Our so-called learned men, however, explain such things by saying that the names of the constellations in the heavens were given to certain personalities on Earth. The truth is just the opposite! Nowadays it is said that John the Baptist was called the 'Water-man' because that name had been derived from the constellation and applied to him. But that is really putting the cart before the horse. You will have heard of a certain savant's ironical attempt to establish that Napoleon was not an historical figure. The argument was that the name

'Napoleon' is easily derived from 'Apollo', the prefix N indicating comparative rank—therefore a kind of super-Apollo. Napoleon had six brothers and sisters and the star Apollo is included among the seven Pleiades. Napoleon's twelve Marshals are said to be the twelve signs of the Zodiac and Apollo's mother, Leto, becomes Napoleon's mother, Letitia . . . and so on, in the same strain!

If we trace the course of the Sun in the heavens we find that as the physical Sun sets the spiritual Sun begins to rise. In its day or summer course the Sun progresses from Taurus to Aries, and so on; in its night or winter course it will reveal to us the secrets of the Initiation of Aquarius or Pisces. Physically, the Sun's course is from Virgo to Leo, Cancer, Gemini, Taurus, Aries; spiritually its course is from Virgo to Libra, Scorpio, Sagittarius, Capricorn and Aquarius to Pisces. The spiritual counterpart of the course of the physical Sun is its passage from Aquarius to Pisces.

Consequently John could say: He must increase but I must decrease. My mission is one of which you will have a picture when the Sun passes from the sign of Aquarius to that of Pisces. I am an Aquarius Initiate and I am not worthy to give you the secrets of the Sun in Pisces. I am not worthy to unloose the shoe-latchet of the One I am to proclaim to you.

In these words John speaks of himself unambiguously as an Aquarius Initiate. Pictures in old calendars indicate the meaning of his words when he says: 'The latchet of whose shoe I am not worthy to unloose'. In old pictures of the zodiacal constellations the Waterman is shown kneeling. His whole posture indicates the reverence he must feel for the Sun as it passes him by and rising in Pisces reveals what is to come. This is the picture of John the Baptist: the Sun passes on and he cannot detain it; he can only proclaim in advance what is to be.

The prophet Isaiah knew that when the Sun progressed to Pisces a new dispensation was to come. This progression signifies the advent of men or beings connected with the

Pisces Initiation. That is why the sign for Christ Jesus in the earliest Christian times was the fish or two fishes still to be seen in the catacombs of Rome. Why did Jesus say to His disciples: 'I will make you fishers of men'? John the Baptist prepared for the Pisces Initiation which the Nazarene had to undergo if the Christ was to descend into him. The events in Palestine, the most important in the whole process of world-evolution, are inscribed in wonderful signs in the Zodiac. What came to pass step by step in Palestine is explained in its depths not through any human script but through a heavenly script which must be consulted for any real understanding of a process so exalted that it is directly related to the Macrocosm. What the physical eye saw moving about Palestine in the flesh and blood of Jesus of Nazareth—was that all? If you remember the indications I have given, it was maya, illusion. Actually the whole spiritual power, the central spiritual power, of the Sun was present in the figure of Jesus of Nazareth moving about Palestine; the figure that appeared physically as Jesus of Nazareth was maya.

Everything Christ Jesus did was connected with macro-cosmic events. Think of how often in St. Mark's Gospel it is said that Christ performed His acts of healing after the Sun had set or before it had risen. Thus we are told: In the evening, when the Sun had set, they brought to Him all manner of sick and possessed. (i, 32). Why were the sick and possessed brought to Him at just that time? Because the Sun had set and its forces were no longer working physically in Jesus, but spiritually; what He was to do was not connected with the physical forces of the Sun. The physical Sun had set, but the spiritual Sun-forces worked through His heart and body. And when He wanted to unfold His greatest and most powerful forces He had necessarily to exert them at a time when the physical Sun was not visible in the heavens. So also when we read: 'Before the Sun had risen'—the words have a definite meaning. Every word in St. Mark's Gospel indicates great cosmic connections between processes in the universe and every step taken and every deed performed by

Christ in the body of Jesus of Nazareth here on Earth. If you were to draw a map of the paths He trod and the deeds He performed and were then to study the corresponding processes in the heavens, the picture would be the same: processes in the heavens would seem to have been projected down to the Earth.

Whence did a man like *Kepler* derive the principles of his astronomy? In his life as Kepler he did not find the powers which enabled him to epitomise the fundamentals of astronomy in his three great laws. These three laws describe in words the movement of the planets around their fixed star. Kepler was able to discover them only because his enthusiasm caused certain memories to arise in him. In a previous incarnation he had been a pupil of the old Egyptian Mysteries. In him, and in many others too, those experiences rose up again as dim intuitions. Such men had in their life of soul much that was an expression of the harmony of the spheres. Kepler studied the wonderful constellations to be seen in the heavens during his life. He observed the conjunction of Saturn, Jupiter and Moon and through it sought to explain the star by which the Three Wise Men from the East were guided. Abstractions as appalling as the Kant-Laplace theory had not been devised in Kepler's day.

The Gospel of St. Mark gives expression to the wonderful harmony between the great Cosmos and what was to come to pass once on our Earth through the deeds of Christ Jesus and the Mystery of Golgotha. We cannot understand this Gospel unless we can decipher the writing of the stars and that requires insight into the secrets of the language of the heavens. When the Gospel says that the Sun had set, this does not indicate merely that the Sun was no longer shining but also that the spiritual Beings of the Sun-Hierarchy had moved into a world of stronger spiritual powers because they must now work *through* the Earth, through the physical substance of the Earth. All this was felt by men when they were told of what came to pass through Christ Jesus after the Sun had set. A whole world of meaning lay in the words.

I hope that these few indications will help us to penetrate more deeply into the secrets of the Gospels. Particularly through the study of St. Mark's Gospel the human soul can rise to an understanding of wonderful mysteries of cosmic happenings. Every word in that Gospel is of great significance.

ANSWERS TO QUESTIONS AFTER THE FOREGOING LECTURE

What is the meaning of the temptation of Jesus by Satan? Are Satan and Lucifer identical? How can the highest of all Beings be tempted by one of a lower order?

Satan is Ahriman. In the Gospels of St. Luke and St. Matthew, Lucifer is meant; in the Gospel of St. Mark, Ahriman. An impressive description is given in that Gospel of how hideous animal forms make their appearance when a man enters the spiritual world in the usual way. There are people who believe that entrance to the spiritual world can be achieved by adopting some special diet and other material practices of a similar kind. But everything they then see, particularly when it takes the form of sublime figures of light, is only a reflection of their own self, an Ahrimanic deception. Both Lucifer and Ahriman are tempters; and Christ in human form showed how man must resist them when he begins to find his way into the spiritual world.

Shall we see in higher worlds those who belong to us?

Spiritual seeing is very different from physical seeing. In the spiritual sense we shall certainly see again those who belong to us. The fact that Mary Magdalene did not immediately recognise Jesus is an indication that the Risen Christ cannot be recognised by everyone; certain powers must first have been developed. These powers began to function in Mary Magdalene only when Christ spoke her name. Much of what Spiritual Science teaches is regarded as heretical, although the Gospels confirm it. The Risen Christ could be recognised only by clairvoyant sight.

Are not the contents of the Babylonian Tables and the Ten Commandments practically identical?

People who speak about similarities in such a case are not aware of the essentials. This is very evident in the case of the Sermon on the Mount. The Bible does not say: 'yours is the kingdom of heaven', but: 'you will find the kingdom of heaven within yourselves'. The Ten Commandments too are fundamentally different from anything previously in existence. Hebraism and Christianity added the impulse of the 'I AM' to what was already contained in earlier religions. When such things are studied in depth they are extraordinarily enlightening.

How is the doctrine of reincarnation to be reconciled with the Bible?

It is not yet possible to understand the Bible fully. Each epoch has translated it in the way that suited itself. The Bible has nothing to fear from the doctrine of reincarnation. It used to be thought that every discovery of a new scientific truth constituted a danger to the Bible.

What is the relation between Christ and Lucifer?

It is not easy to explain this briefly. We have often spoken of how man has passed from incarnation to incarnation and how the Luciferic power took root in very early times in the astral body and Ahriman later on in the etheric body. With the coming of Christ all this acquired a new meaning. We are only at the beginning of Christian evolution. If the Gospels are understood they make it clear that Christ was obliged to deal with Lucifer and Ahriman. But there are very few who realise to-day that the stories of the Temptation differ in the Gospels of St. Matthew, St. Mark and St. Luke. Occultists know that there is not only a Luciferic temptation by way of man's desires, but also an Ahrimanic temptation— when a man carries his own passions out into the Macrocosm and sees all manner of animal figures and forms. The Gospel of St. Matthew describes a Luciferic temptation: in the Gospel of St. Mark, Jesus is 'with the wild beasts' of human nature. In all occult writings Lucifer is pictured as a serpent, Ahriman as a hound.

These stories of the Temptation point to deep mysteries. Just as the advent of the Luciferic and Ahrimanic powers was a necessity in order that man might become a free, independent being, so he must tear himself away from them again through the power of Christ in his soul. The spheres of Lucifer and Ahriman will gradually be reversed. Men will take the Christ Impulse into themselves, confronting Ahriman in the outside world. Up to now, and at present, the opposite has been the case. Such things can be studied in *The Portal of Initiation*. You should pay attention to the vowel sounds. These things are in accordance with an inner necessity. The verses in the first part change in the second into their opposite. This is intentional.

Question not recorded.

It is true that Jesus did not write anything. There is actually a theologian who discusses whether He could write at all!—In four hundred years people will call what is said nowadays about Copernicus and Galileo a modern form of mythology. Theosophists of all people should not talk about 'Ptolemaic childishness'.

A question about the authenticity of the writings of Dionysius.

It is usual nowadays to regard the actual writer as more important than the spiritual originator and inspirer. (Rudolf Steiner here referred to his own experience in connection with Goethe's prose-hymn, *Nature*, the authorship of which had been disputed by some philologists.) Dionysius, the disciple of the Apostle Paul, actually wrote nothing down because in those days to have done so would have seemed unimportant. But his successors, who, as was

customary in those times, were also called Dionysius,
presented a faithful account of his teachings as handed
down by tradition. These were the writings of the so-called
pseudo-Dionysius.

To 'believe in good faith' is not enough; everyone should
convince himself of the truth. People to-day have no conception of what is possible and what is impossible. Things
become tragic in this respect when, for instance, the Bible is
ruthlessly analysed by scholars. Erudition and nonsense
often go hand in hand!

Can Christ Jesus appear to men on Earth?

In the way in which He appeared to St. Paul, this is
possible. When this happens it is a kind of Initiation which
can sometimes take place without previous training. From
the middle of the twentieth century onwards many people
will have this experience.

THE VOICE OF THE ANGELOS AND THE
SPEECH OF THE EXOUSIAI

Let us take as a starting-point these words in St. Mark's Gospel: 'Behold I send my Angel (messenger) before thee who shall prepare thy way before thee. The voice of one preaching (crying) in the wilderness.' In the original text the words are: It is a voice of one crying in the solitude.

Anyone who reads these words with an open mind will at first be at a loss for an explanation. He will regard them more or less as a phrase or at most as allegorical. For what would be the point of preaching in a wilderness? It would be usual, surely, to go where there are plenty of people, not into a wilderness!

In the light of Spiritual Science the depth of the wisdom contained in every word of the Holy Scriptures is revealed in this passage. We shall find that every word in the original text is at its proper place, and moreover is only then intelligible.

What is meant by the words: 'I send my Angel before thee, who shall prepare thy way before thee'? We know that the Bible is here referring to John the Baptist. But to understand why the word 'Angel' is used we must go back to conditions in an earlier period of our Earth's evolution and consider what ranks of Beings belonged to it. We know that on our physical Earth too there is a certain hierarchical order of which the mineral kingdom is the lowest stage; then come the plant and animal kingdoms and, at the highest stage, man. Beyond man is the hierarchy of the Angels, Archangels and Archai (Spirits of Personality, or Principalities); then the hierarchy of the Exousiai (Spirits of Form, or Powers), the Dynameis (Spirits of Movement, or Mights, also Virtues), and the Kyriotetes (Spirits of Wisdom, or Dominions); then the highest hierarchy of Thrones, Cherubim and Seraphim.

All these hierarchies too are involved in a constant process of evolution. Just as we are nowadays passing through the human stage of evolution on the Earth, the Angels passed through the human stage (though in a different form from ours) during the Old Moon evolutionary period, the previous condition of our planet. They are therefore a stage ahead of us. Just as one of our tasks on Earth is to lead and guide our children, so the task of the Angels is to lead and guide humanity. But because it is impossible for them to incarnate in the forms of earthly existence, to be able to help us they must allow their wisdom to flow into the bodies of the purest, most highly developed men, in order that the divine truths may be proclaimed to humanity through their mouths. In such a case we may say: the Angels clothe themselves in maya.

This becomes still more intelligible if we go back to times of remote antiquity and picture the seven Rishis of India. If we had looked at their outer forms we should have seen simple men, perhaps peasants. The essential core of their being was concealed within them. Clairvoyantly, however, we should have seen them in flaming auras, from which warmth radiated into their surroundings. But in order that the greatest cosmic wisdom might penetrate into them it was necessary for all the seven to be together. Divinity played upon them as if they were a scale of seven tones. The language they spoke would have seemed to us nothing but unintelligible sounds.

It is hardly possible nowadays to form any idea of the nature of language in those ancient times because our own, by contrast, is a conglomeration of lifeless ideas which we employ to reach a logical conclusion. In the days of the Rishis it was the *sound* that caused pictures to rise up before the inner eye. What, then, was the original source of language? The wise men, the sages, of ancient times, brought it down from the stars. For them the Zodiac was the

script of the Godhead in the heavens. The zodiacal constellations created the consonants, the planets created the
vowels, and according to how the planets altered their courses
in the Zodiac the sages interpreted the various meanings of
the heavenly wisdom.

The bodies of the Rishis were maya, enshrining the
inmost core of Divinity.

If we direct the light gained from Spiritual Science upon
the words of the Bible, all the bleakness with which materialists are so prone to invest them, disappears. We understand
the real meaning of the words which say that God sent an
Angel in advance, to prepare the way of the one who was to
come. The Angel is a more highly developed Being of the
hierarchy of the rank immediately above man, a Being who
sheathed his spirit in the maya of a human body—in this
case in the body of John the Baptist, the reincarnated
Elijah. If we are to understand the words of the Bible truly,
it is only a matter of shedding the right light upon them and
interpreting them literally.

Theologians are baffled by the words about the voice of a
preacher in the wilderness, the voice of one crying in the
wilderness. What can this mean?

John the Baptist baptised with water. In this baptism the
whole body was plunged into the Jordan as part of the rites
of Initiation. Why was this done? Because the etheric body
of a spiritually developed man was to be loosened for a short
time from the physical body; the man then experienced
what one who is dying experiences when his etheric body is
loosened from the physical. A picture of his present incarnation back to his birth is unrolled before him in all detail as a
kind of panorama and he feels and knows that outside his
body of flesh he is a spiritual being.

Anyone who had returned to his physical body after this
experience during baptism was henceforth inwardly different
from other men: he felt as if he were standing alone with this
expansion of knowledge, separated from the rest of humanity;
he felt that men could no longer understand him, that he was

isolated, as it were in a 'wilderness', in solitude. And in this state of deepest inner isolation he became aware of the 'voice of one crying'—his Angel. In this case the guiding Angel was clothed in the person of John the Baptist. That is the meaning of the passage in the Bible about the voice calling, or crying, in the wilderness.

Later in St. Mark's Gospel, where Christ is proclaiming the highest wisdom in the schools, the words are: 'And they were astonished at His teaching: for He taught them as one that had authority, and not as the scribes.' What does speaking 'with authority' mean? Just as Angels are the guides of individual men and Archangels of whole peoples, so there are other, still higher Beings who are the guides of the forces and powers of nature. These are the sources upon which men of genius draw to create their masterpieces. The works of Leonardo da Vinci, Michelangelo, Raphael, give expression to the powers of nature.

To picture where these powers of nature are made manifest let us imagine that we are standing on the heights of a Swiss mountain. If we are fortunate enough to be there at sunrise, we shall be overwhelmed by the magic and sublimity of this spectacle of nature, and we shall feel pervaded through and through by the mighty forces radiating from it and revealing to us the power of Almighty God. We watch how from the glimmering grey of dawn the first delicate colours of the rising sun appear, how the peaks of the snow-capped mountains are suffused with rosy mauve, and our eyes are dazzled by this spectacle of greater and greater brilliance. We see how the rays call forth colours which seem to stream from every side, filling more and more of the space around us, until finally the sun appears in all its splendour, kindling life and radiating warmth into the lowest valleys. In this majestic manifestation of nature we are actually beholding the confluence of spiritual forces and these forces are the Beings of the Hierarchies we have learnt to know as the Exousiai, the Powers, or Spirits of Form. In the original text the words are: 'He taught as the Exousiai teach.' Christ spoke with the powers of these Beings. In John the Baptist it was the Angel, the Being of the rank immediately above man, who spoke. In Christ it was the Exousiai, who as I have said, speak through events of nature. It was their forces in the body of Christ which enabled Him to teach 'with authority'.

John the Baptist had received the highest Initiation connected with the constellation of Aquarius. In old maps of the Zodiac the sign depicting Aquarius is a man stooping down with the arms held in a particular position. This illustrates the words in St. Mark's Gospel: 'There cometh after me one mightier than I, the latchet of whose shoes I am not worthy to stoop down and unloose.'

Complete Edition of the works of Rudolf Steiner in German, published by the Rudolf Steiner Verlag, Dornach, Switzerland, by whom all rights are reserved.

Writings

1. Works written between 1883 and 1925
2. Essays and articles written between 1882 and 1925
3. Letters, drafts, manuscripts, fragments, verses, inscriptions, meditative sayings, etc.

Lectures

1. Public Lectures
2. Lectures to Members of the Anthroposophical Society on general anthroposophical subjects.
   Lectures to Members on the history of the Anthroposophical Movement and Anthroposophical Society
3. Lectures and Courses on special branches of work:
   Art: Eurythmy, Speech and Drama, Music, Visual Arts, History of Art
   Education
   Medicine and Therapy
   Science
   Sociology and the Threefold Social Order
   Lectures given to Workmen at the Goetheanum

The total number of lectures amount to some six thousand, shorthand reports of which are available in the case of the great majority.

Reproductions and Sketches

Paintings in water colour, drawings, coloured diagrams, Eurythmy forms, etc.

When the Edition is complete the number of volumes, each of a considerable size, will amount to several hundreds. A full and detailed Bibliographical Survey, with subjects, dates and places where the lectures were given is available. All the volumes can be obtained from the Rudolf Steiner Press in London as well as directly from the Rudolf Steiner Verlag, Dornach, Switzerland.

Works by Rudolf Steiner:

Occult Science—an Outline
Christianity as Mystical Fact and the Mysteries of Antiquity
Knowledge of the Higher Worlds and its Attainment
*Theosophy: an Introduction to the Supersensible Knowledge of the
World and the Destination of Man*

Lecture Courses include the following:

The Gospel of St. John (Hamburg, 1908)
The Apocalypse of St. John (Nürnburg, 1908)
The Gospel of St. John and Its Relation to the Other Gospels (Cassel,
1909)
The Gospel of St. Luke (Basle, 1909)
Deeper Secrets of Human History in the Light of the Gospel of St. Matthew
(Berlin, 1909)
The Gospel of St. Matthew (Berne, 1910)
Genesis: Secrets of the Bible Story of Creation (Munich, 1910)
The Gospel of St. Mark (Basle, 1912)
From Jesus to Christ (Carlsruhe, 1911)
The Spiritual Guidance of Man and of Mankind (Copenhagen,
1911)
Karmic Relationships: Esoteric Studies, Vol. VIII (Torquay and
London, 1924)
Rosicrucianism and Modern Initiation (Dornach, 1924)
Macrocosm and Microcosm (Vienna, 1910)

Catalogues of all the published works of Rudolf Steiner in
print, in English translation, also the works of other authors on
Anthroposophy, can be obtained from:

Rufolf Steiner Press and Bookshop,   Rudolf Steiner Bookshop,
38, Museum Street,   35, Park Road,
London WC1A 1LP   London NW1 6XT